CONTENTS

ACKNOWLEDGEMENTS   iv

ABOUT THIS BOOK   v

Unit 1   WHAT IS A TRAVELLER?   1
What is Travel For?   Keith Waterhouse
25 Excuses for Staying Put   Keith Waterhouse

Unit 2   THE ARMCHAIR TRAVELLER   13
Phrase and Fable   Alice Thomas Ellis

Unit 3   ADVICE FOR TRAVELLERS (1)   19
Travel: A Moral Primer   Simon Raven

Unit 4   ADVICE FOR TRAVELLERS (2)   27
Third World Driving Hints and Tips   P.J. O'Rourke

Unit 5   AUSTRALIA   37
Neighbours with a Koala   Sue Copsey

Unit 6   SPAIN   42
Tourist Attractions   Christopher Mills

Unit 7   INDIA   54
An Indian Journey   Jan Morris

Unit 8   ITALY   63
The Volcano   John Stewart Collis

Unit 9   TURKEY   71
Two Guides to Turkey   Daniel Farson

Unit 10   AFRICA   79
Chameleons   Edward Theberton

Unit 11   CHINA   87
Flying to China   Colin Thubron

Unit 12   JAMAICA   94
No Refuge for Rastas   Zenga Longmore

FOLLOW UP ASSIGNMENTS   103

FURTHER READING   106

ACKNOWLEDGEMENTS

The author and the publishers are grateful to the following for permission to reproduce extracts and photographs:

Collins, *The Spectator Book of Travel Writing: Views from Abroad*; David and Charles, 'Tourist Attractions' from *The Sunday Times Travel Book Three*; Hamish Hamilton, *Take a Spare Truss: Tips for Nineteenth-Century Travellers*; Hodder and Stoughton, 'What is Travel For?' and '25 Excuses for Staying Put' from *The Theory and Practice of Travel*; ILEA English Centre, 'A Letter to Jo in America' from *City Lines*; Longman, *Hazard Geography*; by permission of Oxford University Press, 'An Indian Journey' from *Journeys*; Pan Books Ltd, 'Third World Driving Hints and Tips' from *Holidays in Hell*.

Unilever plc page 55 (top); Christian Aid page 55 (bottom); Exodus page 43; The Government of India Tourist Board page 54; Hayes and Jarvis pages 43, 44; ILG Travel Ltd pages 4, 42, 44, 45; Jamaican Tourist Board page 99; Jarrold Colour Publications page 37; Kuoni Worldwide Travel pages 19, 43; by permission of Oxford University Press page 37; Philippine Department of Tourism page 63; Picturepoint page 64; Punch pages 33, 34; Sealink UK Ltd pages 5, 45; Thomsons Tour Operators page 45.

Every effort has been made to contact copyright holders and we apologise if any have been overlooked.

Wish You Were Here

An Anthology of Travel Writing

Nigel Kent

Head of English, Cheltenham Bournside School

Stanley Thornes (Publishers) Ltd

First published in 1990 by:
Stanley Thornes (Publishers) Ltd
Old Station Drive
Leckhampton
CHELTENHAM GL53 0DN
England

British Library Cataloguing in Publication Data

Kent, Nigel
    Wish you — an anthology of travel writing.
    1. English literature. Special subjects: Travel.
    Composition
    I. Title
    808.06690121

    ISBN 0–7487–0493–0

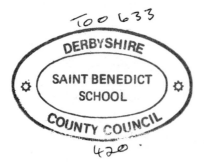
Typeset by Tech-Set, Gateshead, Tyne & Wear.
Printed and bound in Great Britain at The Bath Press, Avon.

ABOUT THIS BOOK

To Teachers   The National Curriculum quite rightly promotes the extension of the reading curriculum in the secondary school. It suggests that pupils in Key Stages 3 and 4 should be encouraged 'to read a variety of genres: e.g. autobiographies, letters, diaries or travel books'[1]. Whilst most English departments will probably have some examples of autobiographies and diaries in their stock cupboards, few will have examples of good travel writing. This text attempts to fill that gap. Whilst one hopes that students will ultimately read full length examples of the genre, their enthusiasm for travel writing must first be fired and this is best accomplished by the study of concise, quality travel texts – examples of which make up this collection.

Each unit consists of one complete piece of travel writing and a range of assignments designed to support the student's critical response to that text. It is not intended that these assignments examine every element of each text, but rather the more notable features.

The assignments are of three types:

1   **Tuning into the text assignments**   These are pre-reading assignments that attempt to give students a foothold in unfamiliar texts by building on the experiences which they bring to those texts.

2   **Responding to the text assignments**   These assignments are designed to enable students to explore and respond to key elements of each text. Students are encouraged to develop and refine their own critical response through detailed analysis of the written word; through collaboration with other students; through visual media such as diagrams and graphics; and through a range of integrated language activities including exploratory writing, improvisation and discussion.

3   **Coursework assignments**   These are written assignments and are designed to produce material suitable for assessment at GCSE. Some of the assignments are based on a close reading of the text and would be suitable for coursework material submitted to demonstrate comprehension skills; other assignments use the travel text as a springboard for the students' own writing.

There has been a deliberate attempt to offer students the opportunity to write for a variety of creative, communicative and informative purposes, for a variety of audiences and in a variety of forms.

[1]Paragraph 16.30 *English for Ages 5 to 16*

It is not anticipated that all students should complete all assignments in each unit. Instead the teacher should negotiate with each student or groups of pupils regarding which of these assignments should be completed. This negotiation should take into consideration the following factors:

- the ability of the student
- the features of the text the teacher wishes the student to focus upon
- the demands of each task
- the relationship of the Responding to the text task to the Coursework assignment the student wishes to undertake.

Therefore, with some students it may be desirable to move straight from the reading of the text to the coursework assignments: with other students it may be more appropriate to move through each of the three types of assignment to provide greater support to the student's response. As with all similar texts for classroom use, it will be necessary for the teacher to judge how best to use this resource and how to support students when engaged in the activities suggested here.

To Students   You will notice that each Unit consists of three sections: **Tuning into the text, Responding to the text** and **Coursework assignments.**

Discuss with your teacher which of these sections and which of the activities within each section you should tackle.

The coursework assignments you will be asked to undertake will sometimes be based closely on the text; on other occasions the text will act merely as a springboard for your own writing. Choose the *one* that appeals most to you and discuss your choice with your teacher. If you are attempting a type of writing you are not really familiar with, ask your teacher for examples of that type of writing and/or try to find your own examples.

Remember that when you are attempting any piece of writing you have to bear in mind

- your reason for writing
- the audience that will read your work.

Both factors will affect your choice of content, the language you use and the way you order your material.

Plan your work carefully as you write and test it out on your teacher and fellow students before you produce your final draft.

WHAT IS A TRAVELLER?

Tuning into the text

Here are five people who want to go abroad. Imagine that you are a travel agent and you have been given the task of matching them with the holidays you have available. Study their profiles carefully and match them with the descriptions of holidays that follow. You will be unable to cater for one person.

THE CLIENTS

Mr Higgs is looking to celebrate his twenty-fifth wedding anniversary with his wife. He wants you to recommend something 'a bit special' that they will always remember. Mr and Mrs Higgs are both in their sixties, and have never been abroad. During the summer they have always rented a bungalow in Torquay for a fortnight, preferring the English climate and having a suspicion of foreign food and water. They speak no foreign languages. Both are in excellent health and like to lead an active life on holiday. However, they do like their home comforts after a strenuous day's activities.

Ginny Dickinson is a thirty-year-old librarian who likes holidays that enable her to get away from it all. She spends all her working life dealing with the public and the last thing she wants to do on holiday is spend her time surrounded by British tourists. She had planned to spend her holidays with a friend, but pressure of work has meant her friend has had to opt out. Ginny is still determined to go ahead with her holiday, even if it does mean going on her own. In previous years she has gone on activity holidays and has learnt to windsurf, canoe and rock-climb. However, she also likes to see the sights and read popular novels by the pool.

Liz Williams and Richard Felton are students in their early twenties who have three months vacation from college and are looking for a holiday of a lifetime. Though they have hardly any money, they want to get as far away from college as possible and do something that is totally different. In previous years Liz and Richard have had to work during their holidays – Liz in a petrol station and Richard in a cafe, but this is their last long holiday before they leave college and take up full-time employment. Liz is studying French and Spanish and Richard is studying Russian. As part of their courses they have both had to live abroad for a year – Liz in Spain and Richard in Russia. They both thoroughly enjoyed the experience, taking the opportunity to get off the beaten track and discover the real Spain and Russia.

Stephen Wright is eighteen and likes a bit of fun on holiday. The chief advantages of going abroad for him are the sun, cheap food and wine, and the chance to meet some different people. He tends to get bored in the daytime but does not bother with trips or excursions. He saves his money for the nightlife of holiday resorts. He also gets very irritated by local customs and the occasional slow service of foreign restaurants. He speaks no foreign languages and likes his hotel to offer an English breakfast and to sell English beer and newspapers.

HOLIDAY A

PERU

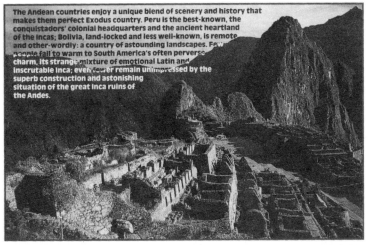

The Andean countries enjoy a unique blend of scenery and history that makes them perfect Exodus country. Peru is the best-known, the conquistadors' colonial headquarters and the ancient heartland of the Incas; Bolivia, land-locked and less well-known, is remote and other-wordly: a country of astounding landscapes. Few people fail to warm to South America's often perverse charm, its strange mixture of emotional Latin and inscrutable Inca; even fewer remain unimpressed by the superb construction and astonishing situation of the great Inca ruins of the Andes.

Machu Picchu

Plaza de Armas, Cuzco

Peru Explorer

Our most comprehensive Peruvian adventure

Designed to introduce you to the very best of Peru, our Explorer trip gives you a taste of most of what this remarkably diverse country has to offer. For scenery, you'll see the peaks of the Andes, snow-capped volcanoes, thick jungle and the world's driest desert. In Peru the scenery is usually laced with history: not dry-as-dust

Sacsayhuaman, Cuzco

Andean child

remains, but ancient cities, buildings and fortresses, often of colossal size, and invariably in settings of amazing beauty. We start with a look at one of the most mysterious pieces of history, a visit to the Nazca lines, which we see from a light aircraft. Then, by contrast, some cities: the colonial splendour of Arequipa, and Puno, a wild-west town on the shores of Titicaca, from which a scenic train journey takes us across the high Altiplano to Cuzco, the magnificent capital of both the Incas and the Spanish. Close to here is Peru's gem, and the world's most spectacularly situated ruin, the lost city of Machu Picchu.

If you like activity too, you'll enjoy sailing to the seabird colonies of the Paracas peninsula, cruising the reed islands of Lake Titicaca, and forging deep into the Amazon jungle by motor canoe. Walking enthusiasts can opt to trek the famous Inca Trail, a superb and not-too-difficult trek along the ancient mountain road to Machu Picchu: by far the best way to see the ruins in their remarkable Andean perspective.

Outline itinerary: Day 1 Depart London. 2 Lima. 3 Paracas. 4 Nazca. 5/6 Arequipa. 7/8 Lake Titicaca. 9 Train to Cuzco. 10/11 Cuzco. 12/13 Jungle. 14 Cuzco. 15 Sacred Valley. 16 Machu Picchu. 17 Cuzco. 18 Lima. 19 Depart. 20 London.
Inca Trail extension: Days 16/19 trekking. 20/21 Cuzco. 22 Lima. 23 Depart. 24 London.
Travelling: bus, plane, train; extensive but undemanding. Optional trekking 4 days, easy to moderate, altitude 9,000 – 13,500 ft.
Group size: maximum 16.
Accommodation: hotels in Lima, Nazca, Arequipa, Puno, Cuzco; jungle lodge; camping only on Inca Trail extension. 4 nights fully supported.
Food: bed and breakfast only, full board in jungle and while trekking. Allow £5 per day for main meals in towns.

Peru Explorer; 20 days Sun to Fri

HOLIDAY B

IBIZA

There is something both secret and secretive about Ibiza. Every way you turn you see something different. Every road you go down leads to a discovery. Every time you go out you find something new. And even when you think you know the island intimately it will keep on springing surprises.

It is an island full of contrasts, with the perfect place for everyone. The scenery is spectacular with rugged mountains, hidden sandy beaches, tree covered hills, cool and green even in the heat of summer, groves of olive trees, vineyards full of birdsong, and always in the background, the bright blue sea.

Take a trip around the island by day and discover small restaurants tucked away in amongst the hills and valleys; follow the bumpy sandy tracks to tiny secluded beaches, almost empty apart from a small bar or café serving ice cold sangria and the snacks the Spanish call "tapas".

By night when the island really comes to life everyone should try Ibiza town at least once. It's possibly the most outrageous place anywhere in the Mediterranean, full of weird and wonderful people, stilt-walkers, street markets, pavement cafés, and bars in which you just sit and watch a world you have never seen before walk past in front of your nose.

And last, and by no means least, we have San Antonio, the Club 18-30 base on Ibiza. THE place for young people. Perhaps the most exciting non-stop resort in the Med. Now read on.

DAYS & NIGHTS

There's so much going on in Ibiza it's easy to put together some really great trips. Don't miss the 'Rodeo Grill', a barbeque followed by the hilarious reps' cabaret and a chance to test your skill on the mechanical bull. A favourite is the cruise to the deserted island of Espalmador where you can wallow in a natural mud pool and dive for champagne on the way back. One of our most popular evenings is the 'Dickens Night' where you are taken back to the days of Oliver and Mr Bumble for an all swinging, all dancing night of beer and workhouse supper. These, plus many more great trips cost around £13 each. Buy the full package and you'll get a discount plus free membership to Club Social and a great discount booklet which will save you £££'s in the resort.

TEMPERATURES

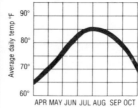

Average daily temp °F

90°
80°
70°
60°

APR MAY JUN JUL AUG SEP OCT

GETTING THERE

*YOU CAN FLY TO IBIZA
FROM THE FOLLOWING AIRPORTS*

GATWICK	MANCHESTER
LUTON	BIRMINGHAM
STANSTED	NEWCASTLE
CARDIFF	TEES-SIDE
BRISTOL	GLASGOW
EXETER	EDINBURGH
LEEDS/BRADFORD	BELFAST
EAST MIDLANDS	

SEE PAGES 11, 12 & 13 FOR DATES OF OPERATION AND FURTHER FLIGHT INFORMATION

SPORTS

AVAILABLE ON THE ISLAND OF IBIZA

HOLIDAY C

S P E C I A L S

Flyaway Special Return Fares are available every day of the week from Dover to Calais or Boulogne. Tickets must be bought in advance and both the outward and return journeys must be specified at the time of booking.

With Flyaway Specials you are free to make your own accommodation arrangements. However, if you'd like to have accommodation arranged for you, ask for our Le Weekend brochure. It has a superb selection of hotels for you to choose from.

Select your flights from the schedules on pages 12 to 17. The fares are shown on page 11.

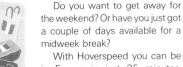

2½-Day Special Return Fare

F L Y A W A Y

Do you want to get away for the weekend? Or have you just got a couple of days available for a midweek break?

With Hoverspeed you can be in France in just 35 minutes, which means you can make the most of the time you have available.

And with our 2½-Day Special Return Fare you have up to 60 hours on the Continent from your time of arrival in Calais or Boulogne. At almost half the price of a standard fare. All you have to do is return no later than the first flight immediately after this time period has elapsed.

A 2½-Day Special gives you time to relax on the beaches of the Opal Coast, or discover the enchanging byways and picturesque old towns of Northern France.

Spend the time in Paris – climb the Eiffel Tower, enjoy the cafés of Montmartre, explore Notre Dame, or visit Versailles; and at night there are a host of clubs and nightspots of every description to entertain you.

A 2½-Day Special even gives you time to travel to the lacemakers and exquisite old buildings of Brussels, or further afield to the canals and windmills of Holland.

You can be as active as you like, seeing the sights and enjoying all the things there are to do, or have a quieter break, appreciating the easy-going pace of life and the superb cuisine of Northern France. Whatever you prefer, a 2½-Day Flyaway Special lets you make the most of the time available.

Now read the following article.

WHAT IS TRAVEL FOR?

Keith Waterhouse

There are those who believe that travel has never been the same since Thomas Cook, in promoting a railway excursion to a temperance meeting in Loughborough in 1841, invented the day tripper. Certainly it was thereabouts that travellers, like the railways themselves, began to separate themselves into three classes: I am a traveller, you are a tourist, he is a tripper.

The tripper element need not detain us long. No longer temperance and no longer curfewed into getting there and back in a single day, they roam the world, vomiting on the ferries, tossing their fizzy drink cans into the lily pools of the Taj Mahal, painting the toenails of the copy of Michaelangelo's David in the Piazza della Signoria. Why do philistines bother to go to Florence, vandals to Venice, when they could spend their money on video nasties and just stay at home? They are the soccer louts of tourism, a roaring nuisance even when doing no active physical damage beyond polluting the atmosphere. The underclass of the age of affluence, trippers, like the poor are always with us. The most we can hope for is that our paths do not cross.

Tourists do at least mean well, even the fabled American who told his wife to do the inside of Westminster Abbey while he did the outside. They go to Florence to be able to say they have seen the treasures of the Medici, not to urinate in the Neptune Fountain. The trouble is that a million pairs of feet a year are tramping across the priceless mosaic floors of the Uffizi Gallery. Venice gets so crowded that the Eurocoaches are turned back on the causeway. Tourists are the locusts of travel, devouring culture and crisps in more or less equal proportions, creating a trillion-dollar industry but gradually destroying all that stands before them.

Who, then, are the travellers? Largely, these days, they are figments of their own imagination – that's discounting explorers and bona fide backpackers on walking tours of the Himalayas. Travellers see themselves on the Channel packet with the briar pulling nicely and a dog-eared *Baedeker* in the patch pocket of their tweeds. The reality is that they are as likely as not to be found cooling their heels at Gatwick or Heathrow, just like everybody else in search of sun or snow. Travellers are, indeed, tourists – but, if one can say it without snobbery, with a better brand image. For one thing, they do not add to the burden of the tourist season: you do not find them mopping their brows in Pompeii in high summer. Nor do they hunt in packs, much less in packages.

Furthermore, they are tourists in the most literal sense in that they do tour – they do not stay put. Whither the traveller goeth, it is not long before he goeth somewhere else, a glutton for side trips and excursions and a perpetual seeker after greener grass. And travellers are trailblazers. Where they go, others follow. Many of the resorts that are now tourist clichés were unspoiled backwaters when first stumbled upon by travellers, who unfortunately could not resist telling the folks back home about them. As Europe fills up and the marble steps wear out, travellers tend to strike out farther and farther: Thailand, Burma, Brazil, Malaysia. But the truth is that they are not, now, usually innovators: these outposts of the tourist empire have been set up for them by enterprising tour operators who in turn have been lured by the burgeoning hotel industry in faraway places.

And why not? Travellers do not want to sleep in tents and wash in streams any more; their pioneering instinct is channelled into checking out the coffee shop of the Xanadu Hyatt Regency for the hordes who will follow. 'Go to Turkey before the blight of tourism sets in,' advises a newspaper travel writer, thus bringing the blight nearer. But of course, when Turkey is spoiled for the traveller, he will no longer be going there. He will be in Tibet. So where the tripper is a lout and the tourist is a locust, the traveller is, it has to be said, a benevolent parasite like ivy, enhancing the host structure (or anyway the host's pocket) but inevitably weakening the fabric. No wonder – to get the quotation out of the way – Robert Louis Stevenson said that to travel hopefully was a better thing than to arrive.

What, then, is to be said for the traveller? What is he about? What is his travelling for? The answer would seem to be that he is a civilising influence – upon himself, if no longer very much on others.

Travel does indeed broaden the mind. You approach a new country as you open a new book – something has to be gleaned from it, only superficially perhaps, but then most casual learning is superficial. Reading Elizabeth David's *French Provincial Cooking* does not make me a cook or teach me how to become one, but it does inform me on the subject. A trip to Brittany or the Périgord does not qualify me to become a guide to these provinces not does it fit me to answer a travel quiz about them, but it does enlighten me a little. The country I know best outside my own is the United States – and all I know for sure after a hundred visits and perhaps a total of two years of my life spent there is that I do not know it at all. But I know some things about it.

Travel feeds one of the most basic of all animal instincts, which is curiosity. Even a cow, which is not very bright, will trouble to lumber the length of a field simply to look over a wall. There is not a shoreline in the world, however hostile, that some mariner has not headed for at whatever risk to life and limb, to see what it encompasses. The traveller, however pampered, always has the itch to move on – even though he may make it a condition that there is a dry martini available at journey's end.

Travel puts serendipity in motion. The art of making happy discoveries by chance is not entirely accidental: the voyager has to set off in the first place. The traveller it is who finds the out-of-the-way village where the smell of garlic-tinged sauces leads him to the one little bistro where the last vacant table is enticingly laid with bread, oil, lemons, a bowl of shiny black olives, and rough wine. But however idyllic and tranquil the setting, however secluded the sandy cove and bustling the market place, however cheap, however unspoiled, it is not the traveller who returns year after year after year. The traveller may be on holiday but he does not go on holiday for rest and contenment – well, not entirely. The village is pretty, yes, a find, yes – but what's the next village like?

Travel is experience. It engages all the five senses. While we may have agreed that the traveller is only a tourist in a white linen suit and a panama hat, here is another difference between them: where the tourist only tastes, the traveller savours. He wants to try all the local dishes, he will drink nothing but the local wine. He will have a stab at speaking the language, and even if he can't master a word of it will prefer to be among the natives than among his own nationality. The Olde Englishe Pubbe, run by a bare-kneed couple from Dagenham, knows him not – indeed, if the resort boasts such an establishment he is unlikely to be there in the first place (though he does not write off Spain because of the Costa del Disco). He avoids tourist traps, even gently ensnaring ones where a boutique selling tat that could be bought in Oxford Street is disguised as the chandler's store or native bazaar or peasant craft shop.

Above all, the traveller finds the time – makes the time – to stand and stare. At the Louvre, the tourist makes straight for the Mona Lisa, gawps, buys a picture postcard of it, and repairs to the nearest croissanterie, or worse, the nearest McDonald's. The traveller takes in all the galleries he can digest at one go, then reaps the reward of the virtuous with a slap-up lunch at a Michelin-rated bistro.

> The more we look at it, the more it is apparent that there is one more comparison to be made between the traveller and the tourist. The traveller has by far the better time. Tourism is exhaustion with little to show for it. Travel is enjoyment with much to remember. That is what it is for.
>
> *The Theory and Practice of Travel* (Hodder and Stoughton, 1989)

Responding to the text

After you have carefully read 'What is Travel For?' by Keith Waterhouse discuss with your teacher which activities to try from the following selection.

1   Go back to the description of the five travellers in the Tuning into the text section. In a group decide which of Waterhouse's labels best fits each person – tripper, traveller or tourist.

   Discuss fully in what ways Waterhouse's descriptions suit the people described and in what ways they do not.

2   In a group of three work your way carefully through Waterhouse's description of the tripper, traveller and tourist. List the points you agree with and those you disagree with, discussing your reasons for your opinion.

   Now together work out your *own* definitions of a tripper, a tourist and a traveller.

   When you have reached agreement, work out a sketch on the following lines to present your definitions to another group. One person in the group is to take the role of the tourist, one the role of tripper and one the role of traveller.

   Each character takes it in turn to define who they are, why they go abroad, what a typical trip for them consists of and how they feel towards the other two types. You could use these triggers to help you:

   > I am a . . .
   > I go abroad because I . . .
   > When I am abroad I like to . . .
   > On the boat/plane/train I . . .
   > I always pack a . . . with . . .
   > The locals like/dislike me because . . .
   > Last year I . . .
   > This year I hope to . . .
   > I like/dislike the tripper/tourist/traveller because . . .

Practise your sketch and present it to another group. You might like to bring in appropriate props and costumes, or you could tape it.

Compare your presentation with that of another group. How similar were they? Are there really three categories of traveller – the tripper, the tourist and the traveller?

3   Read Keith Waterhouse's article '25 Excuses for Staying Put'.

   **25 EXCUSES FOR STAYING PUT**

Keith Waterhouse

You could be bumped off the flight –
    That's if the airline computer has ever heard of you.
    The air traffic controllers at Barcelona could be on strike.
    The luggage tags for Geneva (GVA) and Guatemala (GUA) are dangerously similar – who knows where your bags might end up?
    Isn't the House of Commons holding some kind of enquiry into air safety?
    And according to what you've read in the papers, we're about due for another hijack.
    Someone might plant drugs on you.
    Wasn't there something on the news about freak hurricanes on the way?
    The neighbours went there last year and didn't think much of it.
    The world out there is crawling with clever handbag thieves.
    It may seem quiet at the moment, but don't you remember when there were students hurling cobbles and the riot police using tear gas?
    The courier might not be there to meet you at the other end –
    And even if she is, you'll spend the next two weeks worrying in case she doesn't turn up with the airport minibus when it's time to come home.
    You could arrive to find a message that the cat's gone missing.
    Maybe your room will still have the builders in.
    When the hotel takes your passport, you may never get it back again.
    Inflamed by the foreign temperature, your partner could fall foolishly and passionately in love with a gigolo/adventuress.

You could be in for a bad case of Gyppy Tummy.

You could get lost and not be able to remember the name of your hotel.

The way their coaches drive, it's surprising even more of them don't plunge over a ravine while negotiating a hairpin bend at speed.

A bite from one of the insects they have over there could turn into something really nasty.

And don't you remember that film *So Long at the Fair,* where Jean Simmons's brother gets cholera so the concierge and her husband brick up his room and swear blind they've never set eyes on him?

Don't they throw you into the stinking jail first and ask questions afterwards if you get involved in even the slightest car accident in some of these countries?

What if the brigands who ambush you and threaten to cut off your ear won't accept American Express?

Then there's always rabies.

On the other hand . . .

The Theory and Practice of Travel (Hodder and Stoughton, 1989)

Using your reading of this article and of Waterhouse's 'What is Travel For?' devise your own list of reasons for travelling.

Get together with two or three others, compare your lists and choose the 25 best reasons.

Then as a group present your 25 best reasons to an audience, in any of the following forms:

a) A sequence of mimes or tableaux, with accompanying commentary, of Mr and Mrs Traveller enjoying the pleasures of travel.

b) A promotional tape for use by a travel agent.

c) A series of cartoons.

Coursework assignments

1 Produce your own article entitled '25 Reasons to Travel'. You can, if you wish, make it a serious piece, or you can imitate Waterhouse's style and presentation and make your points through humour.

2 Waterhouse is rather rude about tourists and trippers in his article. If you consider yourself a tourist or a tripper rather than a traveller, try writing a letter to him defending people like yourself.

3 If you have been lucky enough to travel abroad, or even if your travelling experiences have been limited to this country, you might like to write a reflective piece on *one* of the following aspects of travel raised by Keith Waterhouse in the two pieces in this section:
   a) How has travel 'broadened your mind'?
   b) Tourists destroy the places they visit. Do you agree?
   c) Why do you enjoy or dislike travelling?

THE ARMCHAIR TRAVELLER

Tuning into the text

Imagine that your school is about to receive a visit from some foreign students from a variety of European countries who know little English. Much of their day will be spent in school alongside you. You have been asked to produce a phrase book to help them through the school day.

As a group list 40 English phrases which will form the basis of your book.

In choosing these phrases you need to think carefully about

- the needs of your reader
- the experience and knowledge of your reader.

Now create a phrase book for these students. When thinking about the format of this book remember that your phrase book will be read by a group of students who do not share a common language.

- Exchange your phrase book for that of another group.
- Try to read this book as if you were a foreigner with no experience of English schools. Record your impressions of English school life as it is presented in the phrase book.
- Share your impressions with the writers of the phrase book and discuss what you have learnt from this exercise about the problems of writing a phrase book.

Now read the following text by Alice Thomas Ellis, bearing in mind your experience of writing a phrase book.

Alice Thomas Ellis

Phrase books seem to be a universal and eternal source of hilarity and I think I know why. Their authors go mad in the course of compiling them. If you know how to do something – for instance speak your own language – you can go crazy trying to put across the basics to a load of idiots. I once wrote a book about how to feed babies – how long to boil their wee eggs for them, etc – and time and again I found myself addressing my imagined reader in tones of impatience and hostility: 'Oh go and ask your mother how not to burn water, you silly thing.' I had grown to picture my reader as dreadfully unhygienic and monumentally stupid, forgetting that I myself had once not known the rules about poaching and boiling and roasting and had in my time done some jolly weird things to some perfectly good food.

This, however, is beside the point. What I was saying was in connection with the phrase book I bought in order to bone up on my Arabic. The author's pre-occupations, prejudices and thought processes are perfectly fascinating. Opening the book at random one finds the useful phrase: 'My friend whom you saw the other day died last night.' This is followed by the logical 'What happened to him?' To which the answer comes: 'A drunken soldier killed him in front of my house.' Then, I think, the author went off for a glass of mint tea because he changes tack and goes into millinery: 'Is she willing to buy this hat?' 'Why is she not willing to sell it?', and then back to more significant matters: 'She was groping in the darkness.' 'I wish to live and die with you.' There is quite a lot of sex and violence here as you riffle through. 'He advised me not to take her by force.' 'I hit him because he did not tell the truth.' 'If he does this another time I shall beat him.' 'He has torn my clothes and spoilt my work. Please prevent him (from) doing this again.'

I personally found Alexandria not quiet (every vehicle has at least two horns in case one conks out) but remarkably pacific and unthreatening. We roamed round the streets and up and down the Corniche in the middle of the night and so, apparently, did everybody else, all good-naturedly, sucking sugar cane or eating roasted corn cobs, or mango ices. I wouldn't idle round Camden Town in the middle of the night, I can tell you; so I don't know why my phrase-book man is so paranoid. He's nervous about health too: 'I feel pain in my tummy when I touch it.' 'It is nothing.' 'I think you are wrong.'

Some lines further on we have the reassuring 'Help yourself to a piece of bread and butter,' and 'Good people go to Heaven when they die.' I can't really imagine having occasion to make that last remark. Would one utter it in a reflective fashion, as though it had just occurred to one, or does it conceal a veiled threat? It is preceded by 'She can not cross the street alone,' which certainly applies to me. Substitute 'I' for 'She' and I was yelling that phrase every time we left the house. Crossing the road in Egypt is like trying to cross the M1 and thoughts of death were constantly on my mind. We are also offered 'You must drive in the middle of the street,' and I can't figure that one out. Everyone drives in the middle of everything and there aren't any rules at all. How about: 'She was wearing her new hat and riding her old car.' 'Never mind.' Can anyone follow the sequence of thought there?

The following is simpler: 'What is the colour of your horse?' 'It is white.' 'Give me a small bottle of red ink.' You can see the madness beginning to take hold. The author is going to throw red ink all over that boring old horse. He's going to be rude to the cook too: 'Who is this ugly woman?' 'She is our cook.' 'I cannot look at her face.' He really hates the cook. 'The cook has burnt the cooking.' 'A fly has fell [*sic*] in my coffee.' This last sentence is of course indispensable if you want to make jokes, only I can't find the Arabic for 'Waiter, waiter!' or 'Soup'.

I keep getting side-tracked. I am now utterly riveted by the end of page 15: 'Do you like it on the first or second floor?' 'We have a big one in the upper storey.' We like to have one downstairs.' 'What happens to your trousers?' I think I can follow his train of thought here only perhaps I'd better not. He is ostensibly speaking of bedrooms which is tricky to start with. Let us leave him in his more philosophic vein: 'We can often (many times; frequently) dispel (drive away) gloom (grief; sorrow) by laughter (or laughing).' How very true.

18 October, 1986

Views from Abroad
The Spectator Book of Travel Writing (Collins, 1989)

Responding to the text

After you have carefully read Alice Thomas Ellis' piece, discuss with your teacher which activities to try from the following selection.

1 The piece has been printed without its original title. In pairs discuss which of the following titles is the most appropriate. Remember to justify your selection by referring back to the text.

> ALEXANDRIA: FACT AND FICTION
>
> PHRASE AND FABLE
>
> PHRASE BOOK FANTASIES
>
> REFLECTION
>
> A ROUGH GUIDE TO ALEXANDRIA
>
> UNGROUNDED FEARS

Turn to page 18 for the original title.

2 Alice Thomas Ellis' text might be called reflective. It is her thoughts on a certain subject. If you have tried writing this sort of essay, you will know it is easy for your work to become disjointed and rambling. How has the writer managed to avoid this problem?

The following activity will help you to examine how she has ordered and linked her ideas.

a) Copy out the following flow chart.
b) Sum up the main idea(s) in each paragraph in the spaces provided.
c) Describe the tone of each paragraph in the spaces provided. These words might help you, though do not be afraid to use your own:

ironic	matter-of-fact	humorous
superior	sarcastic	facetious
reflective	tongue-in-cheek	contemptuous

d) List the words or phrases which link each succeeding paragraph with its predecessor – for example look for words or phrases in paragraph two that link it with paragraph one and list them in the box between paragraphs one and two.

Examine your flow chart carefully and explain how Alice Thomas Ellis stops her piece from becoming disjointed.

- How has she linked her paragraphs?
- How has she ordered them?

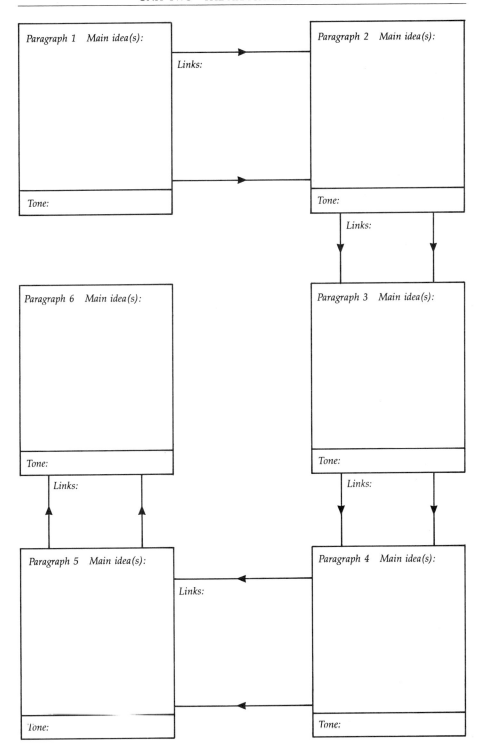

3 Alice Thomas Ellis suggests that a phrase book can give a very misleading impression of a foreign country, but how does a stranger to a country acquire an accurate impression of that country without visiting it themselves?

Here are some sources of information. Working in groups, put them in order of usefulness:

a holiday brochure
travel writing
geography book
a friend's holiday photographs
a TV documentary
a history book
a phrase book
newspaper stories
a pen friend.

Compare your list with another group's and share your justification.

Coursework assignments

1 Create a booklet for foreign teenage tourists which gives an accurate impression of the town/city/village in which you live.

Your booklet will include both text and illustrations.

You should concentrate on selecting the content, language, structure and layout of your booklet to appeal to your teenage audience.

2 From your local library try to find a phrase book for a country not frequently visited by Europeans. Write a reflective piece of writing yourself in the manner of Alice Thomas Ellis, describing the impressions of the country that you get when you read the book.

3 Choose one of the sources of information listed in Task 3 and find an example of such material which describes your own home town/city/county. Write a detailed criticism that explores the limitations of your selected source. You might also examine the reasons why your source presents only a partial picture.

Solution to Task 1, page 16

The correct title is PHRASE AND FABLE.

ADVICE FOR TRAVELLERS (1)

Tuning into the text

NORTH WEST FRONTIER

Rawalpindi ● Peshawar ● Swat ● Chilas ● Gilgit ● Karimabad ● Lahore

*T*he North West Frontier – the name evokes the romance of the past – imperial glory, deeds of military daring, and the high and lonely places of the world. This is an adventure into the mountains and valleys of this crossroads of the Middle East and Asia. From the Moghul monuments of Lahore to the towering snow-capped Karakoram mountains, the colours and contrasts will entrance and leave indelible memories.

Worldwise

Tourism here is still relatively undeveloped – guides are helpful yet not formally trained, and although hotels in the major cities are of an international standard, this is not the case in Swat, Gilgit and Karimabad where accommodation used is the best available. Though passing spectacular scenery, the distance covered by road is extensive especially if the Gilgit to 'Pindi journey is not by air. It should also be stressed that altitudes of up to 9,000 ft. are reached. Pakistan is a moslem country – the import of alcohol is strictly prohibited, and conservative dress is recommended.

Dear Marj

    I don't know what to do. For weeks, I have been planning to go to Pakistan for a while. I got this travel brochure and it looks fantastic. The thought of actually living there for a while kept me going through my exams but now my parents have found out and say that I can't go.

    For weeks, my friend and I have saved up and planned our route. I know it was probably wrong to keep the trip a secret from my parents, but I just knew what their reaction would be. They want me to go on some crummy package tour with them. I'm fed up of having my life arranged for me. I want adventure. I want to see the world and you don't see the world lying by the side of a hotel swimming pool drinking lukewarm Coke all day, do you? I want to be a traveller not a tourist. I want to experience a foreign culture at first hand; I want to know what it is like to live like a Pakistani. If you go to a holiday resort in Europe, you might just as well be in England; you start the day with an English breakfast; you're surrounded by Brits frying in the sun on the beach; you have tea and cakes at four o'clock and you end the day with your mum and dad in a pub!

    They keep on at me all the time, trying to frighten me off the idea. They say the £200 I've saved isn't enough and anything could happen to me during the three months we plan to stay there. They just ignore me when I tell them that if we run short we can always get a job out there, picking tea or something! Anyway, I've heard that if you're clever and you don't do it openly, you can do a bit of black market sterling trading, so that your money goes further! I said that to mum and she went really mad. She's convinced I'll land up in jail or something.

    What it boils down to is that they just don't trust me. My dad says I'm "too young and vulnerable". It's not as if I'm going on my own, and I am seventeen!

    How am I going to change their minds?

        Yours Kelly

        Kelly Mason.

In your group discuss the following questions:

- Should Kelly be allowed to go?
- Do you agree with Kelly's statements about package tours?
- What do you think is the purpose of going abroad for a holiday?
- What do you think is the difference between a traveller and a tourist?
- Do you think it is possible for a visitor to Pakistan to learn what it is like to live 'like a Pakistani'?
- What impression do you get of her travel plans?
- What advice would you give Kelly if you were Marj?

Now as you read Simon Raven's 'Travel: A Moral Primer', try to think what his advice to Kelly would be.

 **TRAVEL: A MORAL PRIMER**

Simon Raven

Since life is short and the world is wide, the sooner you start exploring it the better. Soon enough the time will come when you are too tired to move farther than the terrace of the best hotel. *Go now.*

No need, you may say, to tell us that. But what I do need to tell you is that you will meet with a surprising amount of opposition and frustration the moment you try to set out. Rubbish, you will reply: more people go abroad nowadays than ever before; never has travel, particularly among the young, been more strongly encouraged, never has there been so much in the way of organised tours and educational visits, of international exchanges and cultural fraternisation. Perhaps not; but none of this, my dear young friends, is travel. Travel is not going on a round coach trip for £67 all in, or spending ten days at a provincial university just over the Channel simpering out platitudes about student values. *Travel* is when you assess your money and resources and then set out, alone or with chosen friends, to make an unhurried journey to a distant and desiderated goal, repudiating official supervision, leaving only a post restante address (if that), and giving no date for your return.

Real travel, then, is independence in action, and as such is detested by the authorities. They don't mind your going (say) in a school party to Athens, because they know just where you are and when you'll be back, and they can therefore permit you the illusion of freedom (thus winning your future good will) without for one second letting you beyond their control. But what they cannot bear is that you should launch off over the horizon as the spirit happens to move you, for then you are no longer to be found in the neat little slot assigned to you, all ready to be bullied and interfered with. You (and perhaps your taxes) have escaped them; their files on you rapidly become irrelevant and out of date; there is a danger that you might actually become *your own man.*

So in order to see that it doesn't happen, the authorities (socialist authorities in particular) do their best with forms and regulations, above all with spiteful restrictions about money, to keep you, if not permanently at home, at any rate confined to voyaging within the smallest possible compass for the shortest possible period – and even this niggardly licence is made out to be a gracious concession. 'Few ordinary people,' the dreary cry goes up, 'can afford more than £50 to travel with, so let us limit everyone to that.' Never mind about whether the Government's excuse is good or bad; the point is that from now on and for ever an excuse there will always be, because it suits the authorities to keep us all mewed up.

And yet, my friends, I have good news. It is still just possible to get going and stay clear, provided you proceed somewhat as follows;

1. Put money in thy purse. Earn it, save it or borrow it (perhaps you have a sporting bachelor uncle or a weak-minded grandmother?), wheedle it, scrounge it or extort it, but make sure you have a sum of cash commensurate with the probable duration of your journey. Although beachcombing sounds so romantic, it rots both body and soul. And don't think you can live on your wits, for better men than you have tried and failed. You don't want to end up selling yourself. Therefore, put money in thy purse.

2. Keep very close about the extent of your resources, even in the privacy of your own home. Parental interference can be quite as virulent as the bureaucratic kind, for much the same reasons.

3. Courtesy requires that your parents should be told you are actually going, but you should imply that it is a brief, safe trip of the familiar and sponsored type. Keep your real route and destination strictly to yourself. In no case take dons, schoolteachers, family doctors or priests into your confidence, for these days such people are quite as officious as the public servants to whom they liken themselves. Always remember this: if anyone at all suspects that you intend really to *travel,* bloodymindedness will blaze forth all about you.

4. Leave unobtrusively, with the minimum of luggage and the maximum of prepaid tickets (always secure a line of retreat).

5. Currency. Let us suppose you have the nous to collect between two and three hundred pounds. Now, although there *are* legal ways of taking more than £50 with you, most of these (health or business allowances, etc, etc) apply only to your elders or else presuppose that you are going on some official or educational tour, which is just what you are not doing. Your best bet is therefore to take yourself and your money direct to the sterling area nearest where you want to be (e.g. Cyprus for Greece or Turkey) and arrange matters there, which will not be difficult. As for the morality, well, bad laws invite disobedience.

6. On arrival at (say) Boulogne, you are now your own master for up to three months. Do not abuse the privilege. Behave with modesty (especially if you are very young) lest you arouse curiosity. Send frequent friendly postcards to your parents to forestall anxiety; but do not give too definite an impression of enjoying yourself, as this causes more irritation than anything else in the world.

7. Return before the beginning of term or whatever. You have, after all, your career to make.

So much for techniques. Now a little more about behaviour and attitudes, this to ensure your independence (see 6), to increase your pleasure, and to maintain the repute abroad of yourself and your fellow-Englishmen.

If you enter a foreign country, you do so of your own free will, and this must mean that you are prepared, while you are there, to tolerate if not to approve the political regime which obtains. Do not, therefore, make childish remarks either about General Franco on the one hand or Chairman Mao on the other. If you do, you will be locked up, and serve you right.

Certain peoples (e.g. the Greeks) are peculiarly courteous to strangers, receiving them all, without distinction, as 'guests'. Do not take advantage of this. Young persons of a certain type have recently taken to exploiting the hospitality of the Greeks and then boasting that they have been over the entire country without spending a penny. Such behaviour is unkind to the Greeks, who are poor, and unworthy of an Englishman. It would also detract from your enjoyment, as dependence on one's hosts can be very incommoding. (Another excellent reason for paying attention to (1) above.)

Remember at all times that you are British. This is nothing to be ashamed of, nor, as things are, to be very proud of. But you are what you are, and if you start pretending to be something else you will become nobody at all. I have a dear friend who once lived much in Italy and flattered himself that he was always taken as an Italian because he was small and dark and spoke the language fluently. Why, I once asked, do you wish to appear Italian? Because, he said, I find Italians more sympathetic than Englishmen. What my friend did not know was that no one in Italy ever thought he was an Italian: they thought he was what he was – a Jew. This story has several morals, but the main one is that a man should know his identity and stick to it.

Knowing your identity, and therefore your nationality, you should not affect to feel, on this account, either inferiority or the reverse. We are all different (thank God) and that is all there is to it. So when you go among foreign people, relish what is pleasurable or excellent, and also take note of what is not. You will never be able to make their everyday habits truly your own, but you can share in them, for the time, and you can understand them. That is enough. The same, of course, goes for their moral customs: accept them while there, understand them, imitate them if you wish. But be sure that it can only be imitation, and that you cannot bring alien customs back to England, except for purposes of private pleasure or reference. In public they do not fit here. The more's the pity, you may say. I cannot agree: we are all (thank God) different.

The simple fact will come out most clearly should you penetrate to countries where the people are coloured. You are not superior to such people; you are merely much richer (or you would not be there) and probably much better educated from the western point of view. They have their own traditions (read Laurens van der Post on this subject) and you have yours; in so far, then, as they aspire to partake in your way of life, they must for some generations be at a grave disadvantage. This is nothing for you to sneer about or for them to resent; it is simply so. If you should not sneer, neither should you patronise; and you should never be misled, by sentimentality, into refusing to accept menial services from them on the ground that these 'insult their human dignity.' They need the money; and if you just give it to them, you insult them far more than if you insist on a definite service in exchange. For while it is doubtless unpleasant to clean another man's shoes for a small coin, this is far less humiliating than to receive the coin as a mere dole. Shoeshine boys have ended up as presidents of republics; beggars have always remained beggars.

9 August, 1968

Views from Abroad
The Spectator Book of Travel Writing (Collins, 1989)

Responding to the text

1   Read Simon Raven's 'Travel: A Moral Primer' carefully. Sum up his advice on foreign travel in the form of a large wall chart suitable for the wall of a youth club or students' common room in a school or college.

You will need to

- select the main ideas
- communicate them through illustration and concise text
- find an appropriate sequence for the ideas.

2   With a partner improvise the following scenes, using Simon Raven's text as the basis for your work.
   a) A student is planning a trip abroad of the type described by Simon Raven. She seeks some advice from an experienced traveller who shares Simon Raven's ideas on how one should go about it.
   b) A student follows Simon Raven's advice to the letter and goes on a foreign holiday. On his return he is confronted by an angry parent.
   c) A student follows Simon Raven's advice to the letter and goes on a foreign holiday. On her return she describes her experiences to a friend. This account can focus on the pleasure and/or the problems she encountered.

Once you have tried these scenes, change roles and work through them again.

If you are pleased with your work, you might like to polish your improvisation and present it to another group or the class as a whole.

3   Simon Raven has directed his piece at the late teenager. How has he done it?

Look at the following extract from the passage carefully. Try rewriting it so that it is directed at parents of the teenager whilst still promoting the same ideas:

No need, you may say, to tell us that. But what I do need to tell you is that you will meet with a surprising amount of opposition and frustration the moment you try to set out. Rubbish, you will reply: more people go abroad nowadays than ever before; never has travel, particularly among the young, been more strongly encouraged, never has there been so much in the way of organised tours and educational visits, of international exchanges and cultural fraternisation. Perhaps not; but none of this, my dear young friends, is travel. Travel is not going on a round coach trip for £67 all in, spending ten days at a provincial university just over the Channel simpering out platitudes about student values. *Travel* is when you assess your money and resources and then set out, alone or with chosen friends, to make an unhurried journey to a distant and desiderated goal, repudiating official supervision, leaving only a post restante address (if that), and giving no date for your return.

Compare your rewrite with your partner's. Together make a list of the changes you have had to make.

What does this tell you about the way Simon Raven has tried to direct his piece at his desired audience?

Coursework assignments

1   Write a letter in reply to Kelly's request for help (see Tuning into the text activity), setting out clearly

- your feelings and thoughts on Kelly's situation
- your thoughts on the nature of travel
- your advice on how Kelly might resolve the conflict with her parents.

2   Imagine that you are a parent who has read Simon Raven's article. What would your response be?

Write a letter giving a parent's point of view about the points made by Simon Raven in his article.

3   Write an article for a magazine entitled 'Tips for the Parents of Teenage Travellers', which sets out advice for parents of adventurous children who wish to take the sort of holidays described by Simon Raven.

ADVICE TO TRAVELLERS (2)

Tuning into the text

There are very few people in the world without a sense of humour, although we do not always find the same jokes funny.

As a group, take it in turns to tell each other your favourite joke. Choose your joke carefully. Remember some people may be offended by certain jokes.

Record your joke session if possible.

Did you find during the joke session that some jokes were funnier than others? Did you find that some people did not laugh at your joke at all? This is partly because there are different types of joke. We all have our individual preferences. Certain types of joke which make you laugh may leave your partner cold.

Below are examples of seven types of humour commonly used by writers.

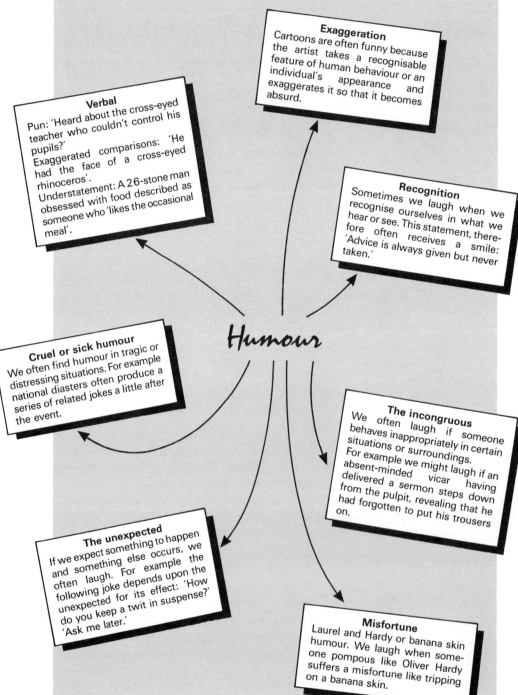

Exaggeration
Cartoons are often funny because the artist takes a recognisable feature of human behaviour or an individual's appearance and exaggerates it so that it becomes absurd.

Verbal
Pun: 'Heard about the cross-eyed teacher who couldn't control his pupils?'
Exaggerated comparisons: 'He had the face of a cross-eyed rhinoceros'.
Understatement: A 26-stone man obsessed with food described as someone who 'likes the occasional meal'.

Recognition
Sometimes we laugh when we recognise ourselves in what we hear or see. This statement, there-fore often receives a smile: 'Advice is always given but never taken.'

Humour

Cruel or sick humour
We often find humour in tragic or distressing situations. For example national diasters often produce a series of related jokes a little after the event.

The incongruous
We often laugh if someone behaves inappropriately in certain situations or surroundings. For example we might laugh if an absent-minded vicar having delivered a sermon steps down from the pulpit, revealing that he had forgotten to put his trousers on.

The unexpected
If we expect something to happen and something else occurs, we often laugh. For example the following joke depends upon the unexpected for its effect: 'How do you keep a twit in suspense?' 'Ask me later.'

Misfortune
Laurel and Hardy or banana skin humour. We laugh when some-one pompous like Oliver Hardy suffers a misfortune like tripping on a banana skin.

Now return to your recording of your jokes and see if you can put them into categories. Which types of joke do you prefer?

As you read P.J. O'Rourke's 'Third World Driving Hints and Tips' think about how the writer is trying to make you laugh.

**THIRD WORLD DRIVING
HINTS AND TIPS**

P.J. O'Rourke

Road hazards

What would be a road hazard anywhere else, in the Third World is probably the road. There are two techniques for coping with this. One is to drive very fast so your wheels 'get on top' of the ruts and your car sails over the ditches and gullies. Predictably, this will result in disaster. The other technique is to drive very slowly. This will also result in disaster. No matter how slowly you drive into a ten-foot hole, you're still going to get hurt. You'll find the locals themselves can't make up their minds. Either they drive at 2 m.p.h. – which they do every time there's absolutely no way to get around them. Or else they drive at 100 m.p.h. – which they do coming right at you when you finally get a chance to pass the guy going 2 m.p.h.

Basic information

It's important to have your facts straight before you begin piloting a car around an underdeveloped country. For instance, which side of the road do they drive on? This is easy. They drive on your side. That is, you can depend on it, any oncoming traffic will be on your side of the road. Also, how do you translate kilometres into miles? Most people don't know this, but one kilometre = ten miles, exactly. True, a kilometre is only 62 per cent of a mile, but if something is one hundred kilometres away, read that as one thousand miles because the roads are 620 per cent worse than anything you've ever seen. And when you see a 50 k.p.h. speed limit, you might as well figure that means 500 *m.p.h.* because nobody cares. The Third World does not have Broderick Crawford and the Highway Patrol. Outside the cities, it doesn't have many police at all. Law enforcement is in the hands of the army. And soldiers, if they feel like it, will shoot you no matter what speed you're going.

Traffic signs and signals

Most developing nations use international traffic symbols. Americans may find themselves perplexed by road signs that look like Boy Scout merit badges and by such things as an iguana silhouette with a red diagonal bar across it. Don't worry, the natives don't know what they mean, either. The natives do, however, have an elaborate set of signals used to convey information to the traffic around them. For example, if you're trying to pass someone and he blinks his left turn signal, it means go ahead. Either that or it means a large truck is coming around the bend, and you'll get killed if you try. You'll find out in a moment.

Signalling is further complicated by festive decorations found on many vehicles. It can be hard to tell a hazard flasher from a string of Christmas-tree lights wrapped around the bumper, and brake lights can easily be confused with the dozen red Jesus statuettes and the ten stuffed animals with blinking eyes on the package shelf.

Dangerous curves

Dangerous curves are marked, at least in Christian lands, by white wooden crosses positioned to make the curves even more dangerous. These crosses are memorials to people who've died in traffic accidents, and they give a rough statistical indication of how much trouble you're likely to have at that spot in the road. Thus, when you come through a curve in a full-power slide and are suddenly confronted with a veritable forest of crucifixes, you know you're dead.

Learning to drive like a native

It's important to understand that in the Third World most driving is done with the horn, or 'Egyptian Brake Pedal', as it is known. There is a precise and complicated etiquette of horn use. Honk your horn only under the following circumstances:

1 When anything blocks the road.
2 When anything doesn't.
3 When anything might.
4 At red lights.
5 At green lights.
6 At all other times.

Road-blocks

One thing you can count on in Third World countries is trouble. There's always some uprising, coup or Marxist insurrection going on, and this means military road-blocks. There are two kinds of military road-block, the kind where you slow down so they can look you over, and the kind where you come to a full stop so they can steal your luggage. The important thing is that you must *never* stop at the slow-down kind of road-block. If you stop, they'll think you're a terrorist about to attack them, and they'll shoot you. And you must *always* stop at the full-stop kind of road-block. If you just slow down, they'll think you're a terrorist about to attack them, and they'll shoot you. How do you tell the difference between the two kinds of road-block? Here's the fun part: you can't!

(The terrorists, of course, have road-blocks of their own. They always make you stop. Sometimes with land mines.)

Accidents

Never look where you're going – you'll only scare yourself. None-theless, try to avoid collisions. There are bound to be more people in that bus, truck or even on that moped than there are in your car. At best you'll be screamed deaf. And if the police do happen to be around, standard procedure is to throw everyone in jail regardless of fault. This is done to forestall blood feuds, which are a popular hobby in many of these places. Remember the American consul is very busy fretting about that Marxist insurrection, and it may be months before he comes to visit.

If you do have an accident, the only thing to do is go on the offensive. Throw big wads of American money at everyone, and hope for the best.

Safety tips

One nice thing about the Third World, you don't have to fasten your safety belt. (Or stop smoking. Or cut down on saturated fats.) It takes a lot off your mind when average life expectancy is forty-five minutes.

P.J. O'Rourke, *Holidays in Hell* (Pan Books Ltd, London, 1989)

Responding to the text

After you have carefully read 'Third World Driving Hints and Tips' discuss with your teacher which activities to try from the following selection.

1   Did you find the text funny? Whether you did or you didn't, the following activity will help you to appreciate how the writer tries to make you laugh.

Here are some more tips by P.J. O'Rourke that have been omitted from the original article.

As you will notice there are spaces where phrases and sentences have been left out.

With a partner fill in these spaces to make the passage humorous.

Animals in the right of way

As a rule of thumb, you should slow down for donkeys, speed up for goats and stop for cows. Donkeys will get out of your way eventually, and so will pedestrians. But never actually stop for either of them or they'll take advantage, especially the pedestrians. If you stop in the middle of a crowd of Third World pedestrians you'll be there buying Chiclets and bogus antiquities _____①.

Drive like _____② goats. It's almost impossible to hit a goat. On the other hand, it's almost impossible *not* to hit a cow. Cows are immune to horn-honking, shouting, swats with sticks and _____③ on the hind quarters with the bumper. The only thing you can do to make a cow move is _____④, which will make the cow move in front of you with _____⑤ speed.

Actually, the most dangerous animals are the chickens. In the United States, when you see a ball roll into the street, you hit your brakes because the next thing you'll see is a kid chasing it. In the Third World, it's not balls the kids are chasing, but chickens. Are they practising _____⑥? _____⑦ it? Playing _____⑧? I don't know. But Third Worlders are remarkably fond of their chickens and, also, their children (population problems not withstanding). If you hit one or both, they may survive. But _____⑨.

How successful were you? Now compare your version with the original words on page 36.

Which is the funnier version, yours or P.J. O'Rourke's?

Which of the techniques described earlier have you used and which has P.J. O'Rourke used?

Now work you way through the original and put in a rank order demonstrating the frequency of the types of humour used by P.J. O'Rourke. Place the most frequent at the top and the least frequent at the bottom.

Compare your list with that of another pair and justify it by referring to the text.

2   Underlying most humorous writing there are set beliefs, opinions and attitudes.

Examine these cartoons carefully, and in a sentence try to sum up the belief, opinion or attitude held by the cartoonist.

'He *loves* feeding the chickens.'

'You know, out of all the animal species. I reckon the human must be about the nearest to us in intelligence.'

What attitudes, beliefs or opinions are revealed in the piece, 'Third World Driving Hints and Tips'?

Here are some students' ideas. With a partner discuss them in turn. Do you agree with any of them, or can you sum up his attitudes, beliefs and opinions in your own words?

Make sure that you can support your opinion by referring back to the text.

3   Bearing in mind the above explanation of types of humour and using your reading of 'Third World Driving Hints and Tips', try creating a humorous sketch based on one of these situations:

- a driving lesson for the potential Third World driver
- the Third World driver in England
- failing the Third World driving test.

Polish your sketch and record it or present it to another group.

Discuss with your audience the following questions:

- What did they find funny and why?
- How could the piece have been made funnier?
- What attitudes, beliefs and opinions emerged from your piece?

Coursework assignments

1   Take an aspect of behaviour from your own culture which could be considered strange. Write a narrative or script which focuses on that aspect of behaviour and which conveys your point of view through humour.

Examples of such aspects of behaviour might include:

- the wearing of extravagant hats at Ascot
- school uniform
- the English love of cricket
- disco dancing.

2   Make a study of the way people speak and behave in a particular environment, such as a school, or a discotheque, or a doctor's surgery, or a church, etc. Produce a booklet or pamphlet for a tourist, who speaks English and would like to know more about the behaviour of the British.

Your booklet or pamphlet will include text and illustrations and can be informative and/or humorous.

3   Interview some experienced drivers about driving behaviour on British roads. Imitating the style, tone and structure of P.J. O'Rourke's piece produce your own version entitled 'British Driving Hints and Tips'.

Solution to Task 1, page 32

The missing words are: ① for days; ② hell; ③ taps; ④ swerve to avoid it; ⑤ lightning; ⑥ punt returns with a leghorn?; ⑦ Dribbling; ⑧ stick hen; ⑨ you will not.

AUSTRALIA

 *Tuning into the text*

Here are four different types of writing about travel. You may have examples of them in your own home. Make a larger copy of the grid on page 39 and with a partner describe

- what you would expect to find in each text (the content)
- why someone would read it (its purpose)
- whom you think it is written for (the audience).

Hold up on the desert highway

S Watts Davies has a cautionary tale about travel in Peru

The Ormeno bus company is supposedly the safest in Peru. The headquarters in Lima resembles a fortress. Armed guards wielding machine-guns and truncheons stroll nonchalantly among the hordes. To be in the middle of this was a daunting experience for *gringos* like myself and Claire.

Nothing runs on time in Peru, so the 24-hour bus journey from Lima to the Ecuadorean border is liable to take up to two days.

Our bus followed the Pan-American Highway. Along the coast the road runs in desert. This is no attractive Saharan landscape, but a sandy version of a rubbish dump.

After an hour or two I fell asleep, only to wake to the sound of a shot. Everybody else in the bus was sitting upright with their hands on their heads, while half a dozen crazed gunmen ran up and down the aisle screaming what were perhaps political slogans. It took me a long time to realise that this was not a nightmare. It was actually happening.

The gunmen were brandishing revolvers. I hoped they would just take everyone's money and possessions and leave the bus quickly. But the bus slowed down and headed off the road and into the desert, and I began to feel a lot more concerned. Out there, they could do anything they wanted.

I could hear the regular "plink-plink" sound of women dropping their wedding rings on the floor, babies crying and gunmen screaming. I hoped they were not the Shining Path terrorist group, who have been known to rape and murder tourists.

After about 10 minutes of bumping through the desert, the bus stopped. Claire and I were the only white people on the bus and felt we were obvious targets.

In the darkness, I was able to hand Claire my credit card, which she hid in her shoe. The $40 cash we had was hidden in a hole in the waistband of my jeans, and our only other money was about £9 worth of Peruvian intis.

The gunmen left the bus, except one, whose job was to clear out the passengers row by row. After a while

he got to us and noticed two white faces, no doubt whiter than usual. He smiled from ear to ear, distorting his acne scars, and exclaimed *"Ah, gringo, et gringuita!"* while motioning for us to leave the bus.

As I got to the steps, another man in a dark suit, with heavily lacquered black curly hair and a grin like a shark, went through my pockets. He found the Peruvian money but missed the dollars. He pushed me out to lie in the sand with the other male passengers, who had been separated from the women. It was bloody cold.

Meanwhile, Claire was also being searched. The gunman tried to put his hand down her pants. She stopped him and he muttered something, then pushed her out, too.

Back in the bus, most of the gunmen appeared to be having a party. There was a lot of whooping, and the sound of objects breaking. I started to feel calmer. Sitting up, I looked around. Behind me were sand dunes. I began to wonder if I could grab Claire and run like hell into the desert.

I quietly called her name, and heard her clicking her tongue in response. Suddenly I was hit by a rock, and it seemed that it wasn't such a good idea to sit up. Then I heard the apparent leader of the gang asking where the *gringo* was.

The robbers began to call for me, so I got up and walked over. They asked [where my] money was. I told them the[y] they wanted to know wher[e] were. Surely every *gring[o]* with them. *"No tienes [...]* assured him, which (alth[ough I didn't] realise it) meant "You h[aven't got any] dollars". I couldn't u[nderstand what] the man was getting [at...] Every time he asked [me where the] dollars were, I kept [telling him] that he didn't have [any...]

Then I heard Cl[aire...] saying, *"No TENG[O..."]* I quickly assured h[im...] no dollars. He [...] *"Americano?"* I to[ld him...] and that our cu[rrency...] He had never he[ard...]

to my story and he must have accepted it.

I was sent back to lie in the sand and they called up Claire. I could hear women quietly sobbing in the darkness, and I prayed that she wouldn't be raped.

Claire told the gunmen that we had no dollars left because Peru was expensive. They laughed. The interrogation was over, and Claire was sent back.

The gunmen walked around their captives, taunting them a bit. Somebody got slapped. Then they all trooped off to the bus, calling the driver. The engine fired, the headlights beamed on, and I was so happy.

Then, as the bus reversed, its back end disappeared down a hole. And here the robbers were stomping out into the desert again, this time really furious.

They got about 10 people up to push the bus, but it would not budge, so after about 15 minutes of this, they grudgingly walked off towards the Pan-American highway, which included their bags of booty, which included my camera from the bus. I assumed an accomplice was waiting for them in a car.

Once they had gone, the women gathered around Claire, hugging her and crying. Most of the passengers made it plain that they were very sorry about what had happened and that not all Peruvians were robbers.

We spent about an hour trying to [...get the bus] out of the hole. Defeated, [...] the driver put

The Independent (10 February 1990)

Title	Content	Purpose	Audience

Now read the following article.

This week our round-the-world correspondent visits Australia.

Neighbours with a koala

by Sue Copsey

G'DAY (Those Neighbours fans amongst you will know that's the usual Aussie greeting!) This time I'm writing from Magnetic Island off the East Coast of Australia. We've travelled over 2,000 km since leaving Sydney but in Australian terms we've merely hopped up the coast! It's difficult to come to terms with the vastness of Australia and we haven't even gone into the outback yet.

As we travelled northwards the weather grew warmer and although two weeks ago we were huddled round a log fire in the mountains west of Sydney, we're now baking on those famous Australian beaches. There are many islands off the coast, and the vast majority of them were named by the British navigator Captain James Cook who charted these waters in 1770. Magnetic Island was so called because Captain Cook's compass acted very strangely as he sailed by; mysteriously this hasn't happened to anyone since.

One day we went sailing around the Whitsunday islands on an ex-America's Cup racing yacht called **Gretel** and were joined by two dolphins who swam alongside our boat. We've done a few 'bushwalks' here on Magnetic Island and have been lucky enough to meet a few of Australia's famous furry inhabitants. On one walk we heard a noise which we were sure must have been a wild pig; a loud snorting and grunting. We could hardly believe our eyes when we saw that the fearsome din was being made by the cutest little koala!

I'm glad to say we haven't met any of those notorious inhabitants of Australian waters, sharks . . . yet! In fact sharks aren't the major threat to swimmers in these waters. At certain times of the year (excluding August thankfully!) the beaches will be full of people but the sea deserted, thanks to the deadly box jellyfish which delivers a fatal sting via its metre long tentacles.

In the next few days we'll be visiting the Great Barrier Reef which extends 2,000 km down the coast of Eastern Australia, so I'll tell you about that next time.

The Early Times
(7–13 September 1989)

Responding to the text

After you have carefully read 'Neighbours with a koala' by Sue Copsey, discuss with your teacher which activities to try from the following selection.

1   Sue Copsey's piece has been taken from a newspaper produced for young teenagers. Look carefully at the language she uses. List any words and phrases that she has used to make the piece sound 'chatty'.

Compare your list with your partner, and then read the following rewrite of the last three paragraphs of Sue Copsey's article:

> Australia is famous for its rich and varied animal life. Most notable on land are the surprisingly noisy koala bears, and on sea the dolphins who will frequently accompany boats for some distance. Despite their reputation, sharks are not frequent visitors to Australian waters. A much greater threat is the box jellyfish which is capable of delivering a fatal sting to the unwary swimmer.
>
> In the next issue Ms. Copsey will report on the Great Barrier Reef.

Discuss with your partner

- how this rewrite is different from the original
- why Sue Copsey's article is more appropriate for its audience than this rewrite.

2   Sue Copsey has been sent by the editor of the *Early Times* to report on Australia for the paper's young teenage readers. From your reading, draw up a list of instructions that he might have given her. You should consider

- what sort of subjects she should cover
- what she should try to do in her articles
- what sort of language she should use
- how she should begin and end her articles.

3   Sue Copsey tries to give an insight into what Australia is like. However, it is a very limited view. What would you have liked to have known about?

Try to find out about the aspects that you are interested in.

Then as a group make a collage that sums up what you have discovered.

Useful sources of material might include:

- travel brochures
- materials held by Geography/Humanities Department
- transcribed scripts of Australian soap operas

- excerpts from novels, short stories, etc.
- newspaper articles
- magazines
- postcards
- someone's holiday snaps
- pop songs by Australian groups/singers
- other travel writing
- tourist guides.

Once you have produced your collage, present it to another group, explaining

- what you are trying to show about Australia
- how your collage differs in view from Sue Copsey's article
- why you think it differs
- how true you think your view is.

You might also compare your views with those of another group. Discuss with them the differences and the reasons for those differences.

Coursework assignments

1   Choose a place which you have visited and know well. Write two articles describing the place. One article should be for a paper like the *Early Times* and the second should be for an adult publication. Think carefully about content, the purpose and the style.

2   Choose a place which you have visited and know well. Write a three-minute script for a spot in a children's television programme describing your impressions and focusing on aspects of the place that your audience might find interesting.

3   Write a letter to the editor of a national newspaper setting out a proposal for a travel section aimed at older teenagers for inclusion in the Saturday edition of their paper. Describe the sort of material you would like to see in it (e.g. What countries should the writers visit? Which aspects of the country should they investigate? Should the material be information or should the writer provide his or her impressions and opinions?), and how you would like to see the material presented (i.e. Who would write it? What style would you suggest? Should they use illustrations? etc).

SPAIN

 *Tuning into the text*

The type of holiday we choose is affected by our personal likes and dislikes.

Here are a selection of photographs taken from holiday brochures which try to promote the attractions and facilities of the holidays they are trying to sell.

Look at them carefully. Choose the ten that are most important to you and place them in order of importance.

'Sports activities'

'Comfortable accommodation'

'Swimming pool'

'Chance to experience a
foreign culture'

In a slightly more modern area of town, but
still only a short stroll from the beach, is
Lloret's West End, build around the "Queen
Vic", a traditional English style pub run by
Spain's answer to Dirty Den, our good friend
Jimmy. It's open late, and has a massive
outdoor cinema screen. Right across the road
from the "Vic" is Rockafellas, the main Club
18-30 disco bar, open well into the early
hours, and a host of other bars and discos
such as the Texas and Moby Dick's.

'Special facilities for the British –
food, beer, language'

'History'

'Adventure'

2 WEEKS FOR 1

Save smart money in top hotspots

PARTY OF 5 1 GOES FREE

in selected hotels

'Cost'

'Plenty of sunshine'

'Beautiful scenery'

'Good beaches'

'A friendly representative to look after you'

A MORE LEISURELY WAY TO FRANCE

Those who prefer to take things a little easier will find Boulogne a delightful introduction to France.

A busy fishing-port, and seaside resort, Boulogne has many attractions to offer. Take a look at the fortified Old Town which dates back to Mediaeval times.

Stroll around the network of picturesque streets full of small shops and inviting restaurants, and you'll savour a real flavour of France.

Or why not visit Paris? It's within easy reach of Boulogne.

'Good shopping'

'Good nightlife'

Now read the following article.

TOURIST ATTRACTIONS

Christopher Mills

It's Britain's playground – a kind of latterday cut-price Cannes, designed for luxury in large numbers. Costa del Sol, mid-eighties – a careful concoction of charms and traditions upgraded into a saleable format for the masses.

Since my last visit to Spain, eighteen years ago, its priorities have changed perceptibly. Flamenco, castanets and threadbare donkeys are now relegated to the second-hand half fantasy of postcards, while fast food, English beer and soccer results phoned direct to Figaro's Wine Bar are today's hard sell.

This visit was an autumn break, planned by the family's women, and I went too. The weather in England had broken, but in two hours' flying time we lost two months of advancing rain, emerging in the Malaga evening to smells of exhaust oil and hot dust, while crickets purred coolly in the airport palms.

The Mediterranean night felt immediately familiar, velvet smooth and wrapped in a composite of old odours – cooking, tobacco and ripe drains. Through scowling passport control, we filed meekly into a dismal hall full of grinding striplights and flies, rescued our rotating luggage and looked around for salvation. It came in the form of the company rep. Her name was Marion – a pale, nervy girl, primly efficient in her starched blue and white, handing out labels, smiles and reassurance like a primary school teacher on a field trip. Hulking porters skulked our baggage away to the waiting coaches under her sharp bilingual command, and soon we were off, already insulated from the country we'd set foot in only twenty minutes before.

My last holiday in Europe was a month in Greece as a student, confronting everything at street level, and I felt slightly cheated as I watched Malaga slip by. Past billboards and under multiple gantries of traffic lights, Marion spoke down the microphone of the city's cultured past, chiefly as Picasso's birthplace. As a backpacking pedestrian I would have found that out at the city museum, or from fellow travellers. Yet this, being a quick and convenient week away, must be a brief, spicy whiff. We were tickled by tasty mouthfuls of fact that had no substance. Nothing was said about Pablo's blue period, or how the light here may have influenced him. My principles were at odds.

We arrived in Torremolinos and travelled its central drag, a long ribbon of hoardings dribbling cascades of coloured light from the mauve sky. It was exactly what I had expected – a kind of up-and-coming amalgam of Las Vegas and the Kings Road, gaudy, shameless and comically misspelt. "Today Specails Onions Omlit – Frendly Englis Grub 500 ptas – Fish Chips at Good Prizes."

Our hotel was by the sea, one of a long row punctuated by palms and dramatic cacti, a series of square blocks washed up by tides of profit and scrubbed clean on the edge of the sand. As we arrived, water was trickling moodily from the mouth of a concrete fish into the hotel pool and the vast creaking succulents by the main door were subtly lit from beneath.

As motley as moths to a late burning lamp, our fellow guests followed no pattern, a command of English being the only thing we all had in common. It was the end of October, and apart from a few family half-termers we represented the season's last squeeze, an ill-assortment of late sun-seekers set on postponing winter. The couple in the room opposite us were elderly, pale, withered and astonished. They had clearly been propped in the plane by a loving daughter who'd sent them off for their first, and possibly last, taste of sun and fun. But they had no stomach for Spain. We saw them tottering along the corridors, wide-eyed and silent, reading off the room numbers like clues in some dismal treasure-hunt. On our second morning, while I was out in the corridor mopping up a spill of orange juice, the man's grey head appeared round his door. We hadn't yet spoken, and now as he peered at me, terrified through his National Health lenses, all he said was "Ants – all over – look." He pushed the door open. His wife was spread-eagled against the wall in terror, and everywhere ants were crawling – over the bed and chairs, up the curtains, in and out of the bathroom. They'd invaded the cold supper the old folk hadn't been able to face the night before. Just then the Spanish maid came along the corridor to save the occasion, bawling unknown arias as she slapped the walls with her feather duster. She took the situation in at a glance, clicked her tongue, made a brief appeal to a suitable saint, then proceeded to wallop her way round the room with little grunts and cries of vengeance and satisfaction. The old couple scuttled away. We saw them later on, sitting in the bar, as pale and straight as chess pieces, sipping Spanish tea and wincing.

Each day unfolded like a page from a glossy mag, a dazed ritual of rising and eating and heading for the paid parcel of beach. Lazing through the vast blue afternoons I read or slept, wrote or listened. Half an hour of quiet would suddenly be shattered by the whine of an electric saw, the lilting wail of the strolling grape-seller, or a row erupting over a Spanish lunch somewhere on an unseen balcony. A barrage of curses and cutlery bounced off the opposite wall in a brief volley of venom, then lapsed. Showers of sparrows rose and resettled, and the beach of bodies turned, yawned and abandoned itself to a further delirium of sun.

In the evening there was shopping to be done, and this job fell to me. Out from the traffic of children, I strolled solitarily into the steadily declining day, along the tree-lined Calle de la Luna, past its shuttered bars and scattering cats. It was a cool shadowy street with a pavement of patterned ceramic squares, sheltered by withered walnut trees and heaped clusters of a kind of blue-flowered bindweed that trailed loose knotted runners down the whitewashed walls.

The shops were on the top road, the main Malaga to Cadiz throughway, a bustling torrent of cosy malls in which I found a small family supermarket full of relabelled imports and large plastic drums of drinking water piped fresh from the hills. The son spoke to me in English and I addressed him in Spanish, everything was slickly wrapped in germ-free foil, and from somewhere on a hidden tape loop, like a ritual reminder, Chris Rea sang *On The Beach*.

This new cultural duality was what struck me most about Spain as I saw it now. We took a day-trip down the coast to Gibraltar, and only then became aware of the huge scale of its adaptation to Britain. Apart from the larger centres like Fuengirola and Marbella the open countryside of scrub, scrawny goats and parched vines is all being systematically bulldozed and built on. Little estates of white Spanish fantasy are creating new and nameless suburbias enclosed by flash-card hoardings in broken English advertising the obvious. There's no connecting plan or scheme. Some of the cheaper flats are plain prisons, the smaller houses self-consciously immaculate, prettily perched in glades of imported forest, sprouting banks of countrified colour from the well-watered dust; a re-creation of Peacehaven with additional patios and palms.

It's the sheer scale and newness of it that unnerves me. Apart from a handful of wrecked hovels in the hills, there's no building over twenty years old the length of that sun-parched shore. Nothing of Spain exists there, and having no history it has no balance. Instead it's a culture under construction, divided sharply into consumers and consumed; an explosive burgeoning of beaches, bank accounts and two half-languages, clipped into rifle-shot phrases for ease of understanding – "Molly Malone's Bar – English Irish Sangria."

So I had learned little of myself or of Spain on this holiday, except perhaps a reflected view of the image it has of me; one of a tribe of beer-swilling, chip-chewing oblivion-seekers.

Yet for all that, there were moments of extreme magic for which I would return. On the morning of my birthday I rose early and went down to the beach with a camera. There I watched the sun rising, billowing up from the horizon at the speed of an airborne bubble, sending sharp angles of blood-red reflection over the wrinkled sea. A jet, climbing from distant Malaga, crawled across the crimson sky like a thunderbug. These, along with other scents and sensations, form the cargo of memories I'll tie up and take home, all of them tenuous and intangible, probably to be unlocked at some later time by the laconic guitar and lost voice of Chris Rea singing *On the Beach* beneath a bank of English cloud.

R. Girling (ed.), *The Sunday Times Travel Book Three* (David and Charles, 1987)

Responding to the text

After you have carefully read the extract by Christopher Mills discuss with your teacher which activities to try from the following selection.

1   Copy out the chart below and list the author's likes and dislikes during his visit to Spain.

Likes	Dislikes

2   Now look back at the features of a good holiday in the Tuning into the Text section. With a partner select what you think Christopher Mills' ten most important items would be and place them in the order you think he would choose justifying your decisions by referring closely to the text.

How does his list compare with yours?

3   This article was entered for *The Sunday Times* Travel-Writing Competition. Any writer who enters for competitions is eager to improve the quality of his entry and increase his chances of winning. Consequently they will often seek advice.

Here is some advice that might have been given to Christopher Mills on how to improve his article.

In your group discuss which items of advice are fair and which are unfair. Justify your opinions by referring closely to the text.

'Improve the title. It doesn't sum up the point of the article.'

'Can't see the point of repeating the reference to Chris Rea's *On the Beach*. Cut it out.'

'You jump from subject to subject too much. It's not clear where the article is going or what it is really about. Keep to the same theme in each paragraph.'

'Why did you bother to include the passage about the old couple? It doesn't tell us much about Torremolinos, does it?'

'You say in your opening paragraph that the Costa del Sol sells its "charms and traditions to the masses", yet the article doesn't show that to be the case. Your account of the Costa del Sol seems to be saying that it has adapted itself to selling British charms and traditions, abandoning its own.'

Coursework assignments

1   Torremolinos is one of the most popular holiday centres for the British. If you have been there, write a letter to Christopher Mills agreeing or disagreeing with his point of view. Make clear the reasons for your opinion.

2   Build a narrative around the old couple whom Christopher Mills meets during his stay in Torremolinos. You might like to tell their story in the form of

- a playscript
- an exchange of letters, postcards or a combination of both
- the old lady's diary
- a series of telephone calls in script form.

3   Christopher Mills' article deals with the changes Torremolinos has undergone to accommodate the British tourist. Here are a number of quotations from nineteenth-century travel guides which also help the reader to reflect on the way travel has changed in the twentieth century. Read them carefully.

English travellers often impose considerable trouble by ordering things almost unknown in German usage, and are apt to become involved in disputes owing to their ignorance of the language.

The problem of the influence of the sun's rays upon the body is one which also needs attention, and it has been suggested that the use of materials of red or orange colour may be of benefit in the tropics in the protection of the body from the actinic rays of the sun which are believed to act prejudically upon the system . . .

A red form of cellular clothing has recently been devised for tropical use, known as non-active cellular. This is well worthy of trial.

Gibraltar is so well known that to offer a description would be intrusive. I shall therefore confine myself to stating that there is but one hotel in the town, where, to use the words of a gentleman who recently sojourned therein, "the traveller will find everything low except the charges." The living is said to be bad; wines worse, beds damp and filled with vermin!

The heat of the cabins is not to be described; ours is suffocating: we have two stern windows, but they are of little use, as, the wind being constantly ahead of us, we can get none and where there ought to be a side-port is a large looking-glass, which only reflects one's dirt and discomfort.

But I could endure all this, were it not for the swarms of cockroaches that infest us; they almost drive me out of my senses. The other day sixty were killed in our cabin, and we might have killed as many more; they are very large, about two inches and a half long, and run about my pillows and sheets in the most disgusting manner. In order to guard myself against them, I am obliged to sleep with a great muslin veil over my face, which adds not a little to the heat and suffocation. Rats are also very numerous. One night Mr. Welby Jackson, one of the passengers, was asleep on the cuddy table, and was woke up by a huge monster running down one of the punka ropes into his shirt, and it was a long time before he could dispossess himself of his unwelcome visitor. The captain keeps a very good table, and has an excellent cook.

> *Good Interpreters* are very important: men who have been used by their chiefs, missionaries, &c., as interpreters, are much to be preferred; for so great is the poverty of thought and language among common people, that you will seldom find a man, taken at hazard, able to render your words with correctness. Recollect to take with you vocabularies of all the tribes whom you are at all likely to visit.

> Without this for the boat on the Nile, a traveller is subject to perpetual annoyance, and to frequent visits from those whose duty it is to prevent smuggling: every European traveller should have the flag of his nation always flying, which will protect him from insult, and save the trouble of going into every town, where he may otherwise be called upon to answer the questions of the authorities.

Simon Brett, *Take a Spare Truss: Tips for Nineteenth-Century Travellers*
(Elm Tree Books, Hamish Hamilton, 1983)

Now produce *one* of the following:

- A narrative in which a nineteenth-century traveller is brought forward in time to experience the advantages of twentieth-century travel.
- A reflective piece in which you discuss what the experience of travel has lost and gained since the nineteenth century.
- A handbook for the modern traveller, entitled *The Dangers of Travel.*

INDIA

 *Tuning into the text*

Here are four photographs of India. Discuss with a partner which *one* best fits your image of the country and where you think your ideas of India have come from.

Now try to capture your impressions of India in words. Jot down words or phrases which sum up your impressions as they have emerged in your discussion of the photographs.

Here are some words which might help you, but do *not* hesitate to use your own.

Now read the following article.

AN INDIAN JOURNEY

Jan Morris

Self-appointed, ingratiating, beyond rebuff, the Bengali attended me down the shady arcade at noon-day. His grin was beguiling but delusory, for if it was partly charm and sly humor, it was partly a native toothiness, and partly I fear emaciation. He was vigorous enough, though. Officiously he dismissed the shopkeepers who, emerging like rabbits from their burrows as I passed, clamorously urged me to inspect their carpets, saris, ivory trinkets or brass trays engraved with images of Agra. Enthusiastically he ushered me down the corridor towards the blinding oblong of sunshine at the end – "You want to see anything madam? I can fix it. You want to buy cheap souvenirs? You want to sightsee anything? Here madam, take my card, I am always available. . . ."

But when we approached the end of the arcade, he hastened slightly ahead of me, and stood there bowing and grinning as though to usher me into another world: and when I caught up with him, and looked out at the street-scene beyond, I found that he was presenting to me, like some Dantean major-domo, an authentic glimpse of Hell.

Across the street they were digging something up, so that huge piles of grey earth gave to the scene, framed still in the dark shadows of the arcade, a background of volcano-like sterility, as though everything beyond were dead. The street itself was all but motionless, for its traffic was jammed absolutely solid, apparently for ever: nose to tail its ancient vehicles stood helplessly there, lop-sided double-decker buses and sagging taxis, the heat shimmering from their roofs: drivers leant from their windows to get a breath of stagnant air, their foreheads dripping sweat, while the passengers in the buses, upstairs and down, were squeezed so tight that they could not stand properly, but were curiously distorted this way and that like figures in medieval manuscripts.

And before me, at my feet, kept at bay now by my ever-smiling cicerone, figures straight from the inferno, Bosch figures, scuttled, staggered and leapt to greet me – men without faces, boys with crumpled feet, women clutching babies like little bald monkeys, old men who seemed to have risen from the grave, children who whined and plucked my sleeve, and scratched my forearm with filthy nails. "Away, away!" the Bengali cried, smiling and bowing still, and so, cringing a little, closing my eyes and ears, I took the plunge into the sunshine, and went walking in Calcutta.

I wish I could be original about the experience. I wish I could say something new. But Calcutta is always Calcutta: it only gets more so. The streets get dirtier, bumpier, fuller. The bustees press ever more terribly into the business streets and the suburbs. The rich men's houses in their walled gardens seem ever more beleaguered. The power cuts come more often and last longer – twelve hours each day on average this summer, and sometimes sixteen ("Milton's mournful gloom," *The Statesman* called it, in its literary way).

Nobody can staunch it. The great park of the Maidan gets browner and more scuffed. The Hooghly River silts up year by year. The civic buildings crumble in rubble and excrement, while swarms of indigent families, counting their blessings, camp in their once-elegant base-ments, or lie about their colonnades. Even the saintly Mother Theresa, in her shabby house of mercy on the Lower Circular Road, can do nothing new in Calcutta, only comfort the dying as they leave.

So I will end with three pictures of a familiar kind – perennial pictures from this metropolis of the damned. The first is a cameo. An elderly, frail and respectable-looking man tries to cross a street. He ventures off the sidewalk into the stream of the traffic, and holds up his hand in a gesture at once appealing and a little grand, as though some remnant of old authority sustains him. He seems to demand, as if by right, the deference that age, weakness and dignity deserve, but nobody takes the slightest notice of him. The traffic does not even waver. The taxis do not even hoot. In Calcutta such a man could not stop a baby in a perambulator: and in a trice, sure enough, he is back on the pavement, angrily waiting for another chance, and muttering into his beard.

The second picture is a spectacle: the Hooghly Bridge, still the only bridge across the river in a city of 11 million people, at the end of the day. It is a burly bridge, but in the sunset it seems almost to sag with the burden of its traffic, its multitudes of pedestrians jamming the sidewalks, its long lines of buffalos, wagons, rickshaws, bicycles, buses and trucks. It is a truly tragic spectacle, as the darkness falls: it looks as though a broken army is in retreat westwards across the river, or a great horde of refugees is streaming they know not where, escaping some threatened catastrophe, a plague perhaps, or a holocaust.

And the third picture is just a graffito on a wall. Calcutta never sleeps or pauses, but there is one instance in this city's life when a sudden hush, like the ominous still we read about in the hearts of hurricanes, falls unexpectedly upon the traveller. It is the moment when the taxi-driver, approaching a red traffic light, switches off his engine to save gas. All around the other vehicles have done the same, and so just for a moment, while the roar of the city proceeds beyond the intersection, you are isolated there in a little chamber of quiet – rather like being in a confessional.

Sitting thus one night, my perceptions abruptly awakened by the silence, I noticed a graffito on a nearby wall, gloomily illuminated by the street-lights.

Responding to the text

After you have carefully read 'An Indian Journey' by Jan Morris discuss with your teacher which activities to try from the following selection.

1   Compare Jan Morris' impressions of India with your own. Jot down any words or phrases from the list above that seem to sum up her response to India. Again, add words of your own if you want to.

In what ways are her ideas and feelings about India different from yours?

Make a list of similarities and differences.

Compare your list describing Jan Morris' impressions with that of another reader.

If the lists are different, try to work out why. Look back at 'An Indian Journey' and refer to the text to justify your ideas and to challenge those of your partner.

2   You may have noticed that the article you have just read is incomplete. The final line is missing. Jan Morris finishes her account of Calcutta with this sentence:

This is what it said, in a carefully florid black script:

* * * * *   * * * * *

59

With a partner discuss what you think the graffiti said.

- You will need to consider what you think a writer ought to do in a final paragraph.
- Base your decision on your understanding and impressions of the text that has led up to this final paragraph.

Compare your decision with that of another group.

- Explain how you arrived at your decision and your reasons for it.
- Decide which group has the more appropriate ending.

Turn to page 62 where you will find the real ending. Discuss how effective this is, bearing in mind the results of your earlier discussions.

3   In her account of Calcutta Jan Morris uses a number of metaphors and similes. A writer of schoolbooks wants to simplify Jan Morris' accounts so that it can be included in an anthology of travel writing for 12-year-olds. He would like to reduce the number of metaphors and similes and rewrites a number of the lines in the original.

This is what he comes up with:

Paragraph 1

Original: Officiously he dismissed the shopkeepers who, *emerging like rabbits from their burrows* as I passed, clamorously urged me to inspect their carpets, saris, ivory trinkets or brass trays engraved with images of Agra.

Rewrite: Officiously he dismissed the shopkeepers who, *coming out of their shops* as I passed, clamorously urged me to inspect their carpets, saris, ivory trinkets or brass trays engraved with images of Agra.

Paragraph 2

Original: I found that he was presenting to me, like some *Dantean major-domo, an authentic glimpse of Hell.*

Rewrite: I found that he was *accompanying me into an ugly and frightening scene.*

Paragraph 4

Original: . . . women *clutching babies like little bald monkeys*

Rewrite: . . . women *hung on tightly to their babies*

Original: . . . old men who *seemed to have risen from the grave*

Rewrite: . . . old men who *were obviously very sick*

Paragraph 6

Original: The civic buildings crumble in rubble and excrement, while *swarms of* indigent families, counting their blessings, camp in their once-elegant basements, or lie about their colonnades.

Rewrite: The civic buildings crumble in rubble and excrement, while *many* indigent families, counting their blessings, camp in their once-elegant basements or lie about their colonnades.

With a partner discuss how successful the rewrite has been. Examine each rewrite in turn to explore how it is different from the original. Use these questions to help you:

● does the rewrite mean the same as the original?
● has any meaning been lost in the rewrite? If so, what meaning has been lost?
● has the rewrite been successful?
● what specific suggestions would you make to simplify the original?

Coursework assignments

1   Jan Morris concludes her account of Calcutta by providing the reader with three pictures that seem to sum up her impressions of life in the city – the pictures of the elderly man attempting to cross the road, the jammed Hooghly Bridge, the graffiti. Try doing the same yourself.

Choose a place with which you are very familiar. Select three or four activities, people, or scenes (or combination of) which are typical of that place. Then devoting a paragraph to each, develop a verbal photograph that describes it in specific detail.

2   The extract you have read in this section is from a larger piece entitled 'An Indian Journey' in Jan Morris' collection of travel writings entitled *Journeys*. The whole article shows that India is a vast country, offering the traveller a variety of experiences of which Calcutta is only one.

Conduct your own research into the Indian experience. The following sources might help you:

travel guides
holiday brochures
geography and history textbooks
personal contacts with Indian connections
travel writing.

Plan a month long trip for yourself which you believe would enable you to sample the variety of experiences that India has to offer.

Write a letter to a friend describing your travel plans, making the reasons for selecting the items in your itinerary clear in an attempt to persuade him or her to accompany you.

3   Jan Morris' discomfort during her stay in Calcutta emerges strongly from her account. The content she includes, the language she uses and the structure of the article combine to make her feelings clear.

Choose a place which makes you feel uncomfortable, and paying careful attention to content, language and structure describe your chosen place to make your feelings clear.

Solution to Task 2, page 59

The real ending of 'An Indian Journey' reads INDIA SINKS.

ITALY

 *Tuning into the text*

Read the following passage carefully. Do you recognise the style of the writing?

Volcanoes

What is a volcano?

A volcano is a hole (**vent**) or crack (**fissure**) in the earth's crust through which molten rock (**magma**) and hot gases escape to the surface during an eruption. Volcanoes often form impressive mountains.

Figures 2.1 and 2.2 show two volcanoes. Notice how the shapes of the volcanoes differ. Mount Mayon (Figure 2.1) is tall and conical whereas Mauna Loa (Figure 2.2) is broader and flatter. To understand why this is so we need to consider eruptions more carefully.

Figure 2.1 Mount Mayon, Philippines

63

Figure 2.2 Mauna Loa, Hawaii

If the magma is very runny then it will come to the surface relatively gently. Once on the surface it is known as **lava**. This lava may flow for many kilometres before cooling and becoming rock. The result of this gentle eruption is a broad, flat volcano like that of Mauna Loa. Its shape gives it the name **shield** volcano.

If the magma is thick and treacle-like it requires a greater force to eject it, as old magma often blocks the vent. The eruptions tend to be violent and the lava, being thick, cools rapidly giving the volcano a tall conical shape like that of Mount Mayon. With each eruption the volcano gets bigger and bigger until a huge eruption may eventually cause the volcano to blow itself up!

Apart from a lava a volcanic eruption may produce ash and larger fragments of rock (**pyroclastics**). As the pyroclastics settle on the lava the volcano takes on a layered structure. This gives the volcano the name **composite**.

To summarise, there are two main volcano shapes; broad and flat (**shield**), and tall and conical (**composite**). The difference in shape is due to the nature of the magma and the violence of the eruption.

There is a more violent eruption still that produces no lava but instead, a huge white-hot cloud of ash and gas is blasted into the air. Such a cloud is called a **nuée ardente**.

Simon Ross, *Hazard Geography* (Longman, 1987)

In the box below there are descriptions of different types of writing, different audiences and different writing intentions. Copy the box and circle the words that describe the type, audience and purpose of the passage you have just read.

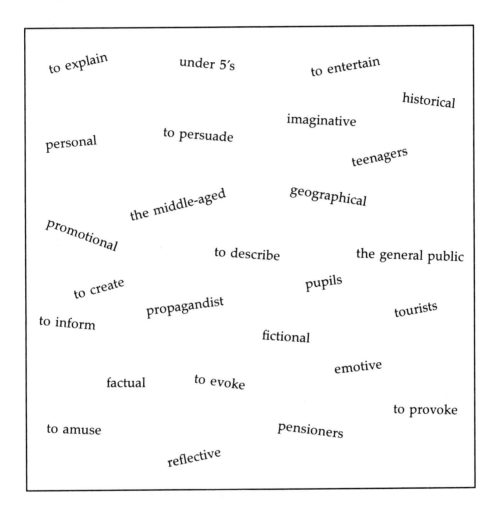

Now compare your list to that of your partner. If they do not agree discuss the differences and come to an agreement by referring closely to aspects of the text.

To explore further what effect audience and purpose have on this writer's use of language, copy out the following table selecting the appropriate phrases from the right-hand column to describe the category in the left-hand column:

Language feature	Description
use of vocabulary	simple, common words; difficult words explained no limit to vocabulary; selected for its effect no figurative language (metaphors, similes etc) some figurative language
sentence length	usually less than ten words usually more than ten words variable – no pattern
use of brackets	frequent infrequent not at all
length of paragraph	usually less than five sentences usually more than five sentences variable – no pattern
order of paragraphs	arranged chronologically arranged to show a contrast each paragraph develops related theme or subject
use of illustrations	frequent (more than one per text) infrequent (one per text) not used

After you have read John Stewart Collis' 'The Volcano', look back at the box on page 65 and put brackets round the words that best describe the type, audience and purpose of his piece.

You will notice that some words in the final three paragraphs have been omitted (see Task 1 on p. 69).

THE VOLCANO

John Stewart Collis

My first impression was of harmony. As I approached the vicinity of Mount Etna (erupting in 1928) it seemed to me that harmony had been established between Man and Nature. Every rock and all the stones, every cliff and cleft, each yard of soil, had joined with Man in the making of vineyards. On the level and the perpendicular, the slant and the criss-cross, grape-vines were succoured by Nature and supported by Man. And sometimes high crags turned into castles, and on many a ledge or shoulder single houses clung like flowers.

I reached the famous mountain citadel of Taormina, separated by several ridges from Mount Etna. Looking south from my hotel window I could see the mountain domed with snow. And there also, even up to the snow, vines were laced. The eruption did not burst out dramatically from the top, but from half-way down the mountain. At this distance it looked in the daytime like a big bonfire, trailing smokingly down to the sea. At night it was a waterfall of fire.

I determined to do two things: to reach the scene of the eruption, and to find what was left of the village of Mascali which was reported to be overwhelmed by the lava. At first I tried to do this on my own, but completely failed to get anywhere near the right spot to start climbing towards the volcano. Then I fell in with a German journalist with a car and guides who knew the right place to go – and I joined them. We drove at a dangerous speed along terrible roads, and through un-motorconscious mountain villages, until the track stopped even our driver.

We went along a path with walls on each side, and the walls, and the groves, ended. In fact they were buried under what looked to me like a huge railway embankment composed of charcoal. I climbed onto it. It did not burn my shoes. This was my first experience of lava. I could see it stretching up the mountain and down towards the sea.

The next thing to do was to follow it up to its source. After climbing by the side of this 'embankment' for some distance I tried walking on the lava again. This was less comfortable now, for I was in danger of scorching my shoes, and smoke got into my eyes. The width of this lava-stream was roughly that of the Thames at Charing Cross. I say stream, for I discerned that the centre of it was *slowly moving*. My part on the edge was steady, though a little hot. In the centre it was moving down. Its red heat could be seen even in the sunlight. I was interested also in its silence, its quantity, and its power.

At this point the guides said it would be dangerous to climb any higher, and the German journalist concurred. So I parted from them and pursued my way alone.

It was not long before I actually did reach the source from which the lava _____①. I could see very little through the smoke which now began to _____② my throat, so sticking a handkerchief into my mouth I advanced. I was near the _____ ③. I dimly saw a _____ ④ of grey _____ ⑤ _____ ⑥ rising from a kind of cave in the mountain. I approached nearer; and now I heard a noise as of _____ _____ ⑦ – sounds of men at work where no men could be at work. I retired through the sulphurous air, catching sight while doing so of the _____ ⑧, _____ ⑨ snow above. I was _____ ⑩ with this.

Now to find Mascali. I _____ ⑪ down by the side of the lava, _____ ⑫ to see what had happened to the village. It was the same scene all the way down; walls, roads and groves _____ ⑬ ending, and the embankment of _____ ⑭ in their place, _____ ⑮ everything. Sometimes a farmhouse would be _____ ⑯, or standing on the fringe quite _____ ⑰ with a tree at the door, while another tree a few yards further out was _____ ⑱ down under the _____ ⑲ of the edge of the lava, whereas the tree in front of it was scarcely _____ ⑳ at all. I even saw, what one hears of so often, a Madonna and Child placed in a nook in a wall, just _____ ㉑ destruction. Nothing seemed to be burnt. This tree would be _____ ㉒, the one a yard away not even _____ ㉓: this house _____ ㉔ – its neighbour _____ ㉕, though pathetically deserted.

As I ran down I could see a long expanse of lava now, a kind of desolate _____ ㉖, so wide had the _____ ㉗ become. If a moor is desolate, what of this? – here no living thing would ever lodge. I saw again that the middle part was slowly _____ ㉘. Near the bottom, I had heard, it advanced a few hundred yards a day. Before it reached a house the inhabitants could remove the windows and doors for future use. Then entering in, _____ ㉙ slowly, _____ ㉚ surely, the monster would deposit itself upon that house, and *bury* it.

Views from Abroad
The Spectator Book of Travelling (Collins, 1989)

68

Responding to the text

After you have carefully read 'The Volcano' by John Stewart Collis discuss with your teacher which activities to try from the following selection.

1   The passage describing the effect of the lava on the landscape has been printed with words omitted. With a partner work out what those words might be.

    For each space find as many possible alternative words that you can. Then select the word which you think most appropriate.

    Remember that each word must enable the sentence to make sense and it must fit in with the effect of the passage as a whole.

    All spaces with the exception of space 7 indicate that a single word has been omitted. To complete space 7 you will have to find an appropriate phrase.

2   When you have completed this activity, look at the page overleaf where you will find the missing words.

    Compare the writer's selection of words with yours. Use a grid like the one below to help you. You will need 30 lines.

    In the *Associated words* column note other words in the passage that attempt to reinforce or contrast with the same feeling or picture.

    In the *Effect* column try to describe the feeling or idea that the writer is trying to capture.

    Can you spot any patterns? Whose selection of words is more effective? Yours or the writer's?

Your words	The writer's words	Associated words	Effect

3   You may have noticed from activities one and two that John Stewart Collis's 'The Volcano' uses very different vocabulary from that used in the extract from the geography book. But what about the other features of language used which were referred to in the table on page 66. To explore the other differences in language use, return to this table and complete it for John Stewart Collis' article.

With a partner sum up the reasons for the differences between these two types of writing.

Coursework assignments

1   Write a promotional leaflet encouraging tourists to visit Mount Etna. Remember that writers of brochures use a particular sort of jargon and seek to promote an appealing image of a place.

2   Take the theme of nature dominating man and write either a narrative, description or reflective piece that brings out this theme.

3   Try writing two accounts of the same place that you know well; one that seeks to convey only information about the place and one that also seeks to create a sense of the atmosphere.

Solution to Task 1 on pages 67 and 68

The missing words are: ① flowed; ② affect; ③ pit; ④ stream; ⑤ boiling; ⑥ fluid; ⑦ men pouring gravel down a shaft into a ship's hold; ⑧ chill; ⑨ fresh; ⑩ satisfied; ⑪ ran; ⑫ hoping; ⑬ suddenly; ⑭ charcoal; ⑮ obliterating; ⑯ half-submerged; ⑰ untouched; ⑱ bent; ⑲ weight; ⑳ visible; ㉑ escaping; ㉒ overthrown; ㉓ singed; ㉔ destroyed; ㉕ intact; ㉖ moor; ㉗ 'river'; ㉘ moving; ㉙ creeping; ㉚ creeping.

TURKEY

Tuning into the text

Read the following advert carefully:

> **Wanted for the month of July**
> *EXPERIENCED TURKISH GUIDE*
>
> Quiet, elderly couple desire an experienced, resourceful and reliable guide with considerable local knowledge, to accompany them on a painting tour of the historic sites of Turkey.
>
> *Some assistance with domestic duties may be required.*

Convert this advert into a checklist of qualities to look for in potential applicants for this post.

Do not confine yourself to the qualities named in the advert. Think carefully about what makes a good guide and the nature of the couple who are seeking the guide. Then list *all* the qualities you think are needed in the ideal applicant for the post.

As you read 'Two Guides to Turkey' use your checklist to assess the characters of Yusuf and Ibrahim.

TWO GUIDES TO TURKEY

Daniel Farson

'I am number one man in Istanbul,' Yusuf informed me when we left the tourist office after he had been chosen as my guide. 'Twenty per cent of Istanbul knows me. I do not know them. Funny! My mother was a countess, my father was a count, I am son-of-a-gun.'

'You certainly are,' I agreed.

Wiry and swarthy, with the penetrating eyes of an experienced interrogator, Yusuf exuded intrigue like a character from a bad film about the Casbah or the Grand Bazaar in Cairo, and I became a sweaty Sidney Greenstreet following in the wake of his Peter Lorre. He claimed he had lost his voice on the new Orient Express, which was hard to believe for he never stopped talking. To Yusuf, interruption was the spice of conversation. This was the first time that a guide had been laid on especially for myself and I began to realise how delicate this relationship can be. If the guide is too strident, overwhelming the ignorant traveller with his superior knowledge, moving at a breathless pace with no time on the schedule to sit down and drink, it could ruin a visit. Fortunately, Yusuf and I developed a sardonic understanding and though this was built on mutual suspicion it avoided the risk of an all-out row. Also, it must be admitted that Yusuf knew Istanbul backwards, at home in the hustle of this tough, vibrant city, a fusion of east and west, with the marvellous, hovering skyline of mosques and minarets, and dark, desperate alleys. It seemed a pity that my briefing was so respectable: old wooden houses and tourist attractions. Yusuf descended with such authority that I wondered if he belonged to a secret international police, and at one exasperated moment I asked him, 'How many men have you killed?'

'I prefer to make crime,' he replied mysteriously. To show he was joking, he added: 'My wish is for the advancement of humankind and world culture.' He came out with many phrases like that.

Nothing was beyond his intelligence, no human experience had been denied him. But even Yusuf was only permitted to hint at the proof in his possession of visitors from space. His reticence implied that he had been involved personally in this close encounter; had they landed, listened to Yusuf, and gone away again? Disconcertingly, his wildest claims proved true. Allegedly fluent in sixteen languages, he really had written a guidebook to Istanbul in Japanese.

'You did not realise?' he rebuked me when I expressed surprise. 'I *am* part-Japanese.'

When a Turkish girl who works in the architectural department of the government brought me a magnificent poster of the wooden houses she is trying to preserve, Yusuf nodded his approval: 'Yes, I took that photograph myself.'

'*You* did!' the girl and I exclaimed simultaneously, and sounded so incredulous that Yusuf modified his claim: 'I held the camera for the photographer.' But I discovered that he had taken several of the colour shots for the glossy brochure of the venerable Pera Palas Hotel where I was given further proof of Yusuf's versatility as he sketched me on a pink piece of paper in the ornate Middle Hall.

'I did not realise you were an artist, too.'

'My pictures are everywhere in Spain.'

'The Prado?'

'No,' he corrected me indignantly. 'All in private houses.'

He signed the portrait with a flourish, *El Turco,* presumably the equivalent of *El Greco,* and I have kept it in case any twinge of vanity should ever rise in me again: the rosebud lips of Oscar Wilde, the mirthless eyes of Edward Heath, and a look of horror all my own.

'Lifelike,' I remarked wanly, with the awful suspicion that it was.

'But of course,' he smiled, accepting the compliment. 'No problem.' As a guide, Yusuf could not be faulted. He protected me from beggars with volleys of abuse, shook his fist alarmingly at small boys who wanted to ask about my camera, bullied the courteous staff of a fashionable restaurant into serving me a banquet on the Bosphorus. He never let me down, until my last evening, when he disappeared. As I waited for him, sipping a beer in that splendid hall in the Pera Palas, I thought I had caught him out at last. In my anxiety when the time of my flight drew closer, I was hardly aware of the discordant music coming from a distant room until it grew so strange that I stopped to listen – someone was playing the piano very badly indeed. *El Beethoven*? It had to be, and was.

'You did not know I am musician?' Yusuf looked up proudly as I hurried in.

'No, but I recognised your touch.'

There was plenty of time to wait at the airport, there always is, and I felt that Yusuf was bracing himself to ask a question. Should one tip guides I wondered, and discovered later that indeed one should, but this request had nothing to do with money. Yusuf is in love with an English girl who worked in our embassy at Ankara – now she has returned home and there are no letters. If 'Lorraine' should read this he hopes to hear from you again. Presumably she will recognise the description, there can be only one Yusuf.

It was disappointing to realise that behind the bluster he was vulnerable just like the rest of us, and it ill became him. My flight was called and I was relieved by the return of arrogance as he shook me clammily by the hand with the firm instruction to ask for him should I return to Istanbul: 'I will be happy to have the happiness to be your guide-friend, and be sure I'll be the best in Turkey.'

My second guide to Turkey proved the perfect antidote. Ibrahim was a gentle man. He met me at Antalya airport advancing with the waddle of a jovial penguin, due to a crooked foot after a fall from his horse at the age of seven. Ibrahim's association with animals has a terrible irony as I discovered over dinner that first night on the prow-like balcony of the Talya Hotel.

A few months earlier he had been told of an abandoned dog whose neck was twisted horribly by a coil of wire. Probably this had been used to tie it up as a puppy, but now the wire was strangling the animal slowly as it grew larger. Ibrahim hired a car, fetched the local vet, and set out for the village where everyone denied knowledge of the dog until a boy whispered that he might find it in a ruined house on the outskirts.

Sure enough he glimpsed a flash of frightened eyes in a corner before the dog made a dash for it, but Ibrahim managed to seize it by the ears. The vet moved in quickly and gave it an injection; they cut the wire, cleaned it up, and when the dog recovered it was free. Before they left the village Ibrahim gave some money to a family to feed the dog, but the vet refused his fee saying, 'If you're mad enough to do all this for some strange dog, I haven't got the heart to charge you.'

Ibrahim was rewarded. On that same day of my arrival a man from the village had called at his office to tell him some good news: 'The dog has had five puppies and all are well.'

A nice enough story but Ibrahim's courage in seizing a wild dog by the ears was beyond a natural reaction from someone who is fond of animals – Ibrahim is *allergic* to dogs.

It started with that fall from his horse which left him with an upturned foot which convinces every dog that he is about to be kicked and had better act first. A bulldog on the boat to Istanbul where young Ibrahim was sent to hospital was restrained with difficulty from attacking him and this has been a penalty of Ibrahim's life ever since. Even so, when he saw a stray mongrel sleeping in front of the wheels of a jeep near his office in Antalya, he did not hesitate to lift it out of harm's way. In the panic of being woken, the dog scratched his hand accidentally but deeply enough for Ibrahim to go to the doctor who told him that unless he traced the dog within four days and found it free from disease, he would have to be given injections.

For the next four days Ibrahim and his friends searched every corner of Antalya but the strange dog had disappeared. So Ibrahim started a course of injections. After the fourteenth his body became paralysed while another man died from the same drug. Ibrahim recovered but he had to spend the next five months at home convalescing. At last he was able to return to work and as he approached his office saw the same stray mongrel trotting along the edge of the pavement – perfectly healthy. His year of pain had been pointless. Today he remains as fond of dogs as ever, but he cannot even bring himself to stroke them. This is why he was so courageous in seizing the wild dog by the ears.

Though Ibrahim could be sentimental, he revealed unexpected passions. When we stopped at the lagoon of Olu-Deniz, I noticed an older man with an attractive woman and wondered about their relationship.

'Eighty-five!' cried Ibrahim in my ear.

'What?' The man did not look that old.

'You stare at her breasts?'

'Well . . . as a matter of fact . . .'

He interrupted me proudly. 'I can always tell measurements of ladies breasts – I am expert.' For a moment it could have been Yusuf.

Ibrahim's knowledge was remarkable, for his education came to an end with fall from his horse. When he was nineteen he worked for an American firm laying diesel pipes across the country, and this was how he learned English and became a guide though the lack of a formal education has kept him in a low grade with a monthly salary of £60, even now on the verge of retirement. Yet Ibrahim is the doyen of guides, a master of his art, advising ten Presidents and the Aga Khan family for the last 20 years. Taking his work as seriously as an ambassador he regards a rapport with his clients as vital: 'People are like envelopes – until you open them up you don't understand them.' He refused to be rushed but proceeds at his own leisurely pace: 'I don't like to be robotic guide.' When a party asked him to 'do' the ruined city of Termossos in an hour, squeezed into their schedule, he declined: 'I have some feeling. I do not accept their programme.' But when he led me there, climbing to the necropolis where ten thousand tombs tumble down the mountainside much as the earthquakes left them nearly 2,000 years ago, he showed the agility of a goat inspite of his crooked foot, resting every hundred yards or so to give me the historical background to this extraordinary place where the people defied Alexander in 333 BC.

It was Ibrahim who was sent for when Prince Rainier and Princess Grace came to Antalya for Jacques Cousteau's conference on pollution in the Mediterranean. First grade guides and top officials flew in from Ankara especially, but when they were unable to answer the questions from Princess Grace the whisper went out to fetch the lowly Ibrahim who had been banished from this special occasion.

'But I am nothing,' he protested, savouring every second of his power, 'I am only eighth-grade guide.'

'That doesn't matter,' they told him impatiently. 'We need you. Today you can be first-grade guide.'

When Princess Grace heard his replies and sensed his intelligence, she insisted on Ibrahim as her personal guide for the rest of the visit, refusing to start her cocktail party on the last evening without him. Ibrahim had not been invited due to protocol, so they hurried to his house again.

'Princess Grace wants *me*?' he asked with humility. 'Are you sure you have the right man?' But Princess Grace waved to him when he arrived, so he waddled through 500 glittering guests to sit beside her at the top table. With her particular interest in the mythology of this part of Turkey, they talked for an hour until Ibrahim sensed the glares of the protocol officials and made his excuses: 'Princess, you are very important person and I do not like to prevent others from seeing you. It is time I go back to my home.'

The next day Prince Rainier presented Ibrahim with a medal, a family album of photographs, and a final compliment: 'If you ever come to Monaco, *we* shall be your guide.'

Ibrahim in Monte Carlo is not an image that springs trippingly to the mind. If he should present himself at the castle gates, mopping his brow and wiping his spactacles, I should not be surprised if the guards turn him away, but I think that Princess Grace would have spied him from her window in the best tradition of fairy tales as he limped down the road, and called him back as she remembered his wisdom and courtesy.

This is how I felt about him when we ended our journey at Marmaris, and when we parted on the quayside I embraced him suddenly in the Turkish style for I knew I was saying goodbye to a friend, as well as a valuable guide.   *23 October, 1982*

Views from Abroad
The Spectator Book of Travel Writing (Collins, 1989)

Responding to the text

After you have carefully read 'Two Guides to Turkey' by Daniel Farson discuss with your teacher which activities to try from the following selection.

1   As a group consider the relative merits of Yusuf and Ibrahim for the post described in the advert and try to agree on which of these characters you would appoint.

2   Daniel Farson not only provides us with portraits of two unique characters; he also clearly states his feelings towards each of them. This activity will help you reflect on those feelings.

Draw two copies of the frames below. Label one Yusuf and one Ibrahim. In the inner spaces record words or phrases that capture Daniel Farson's feelings for each guide and in the outer space write words or phrases from the text that capture those feelings.

YUSUF   IBRAHIM

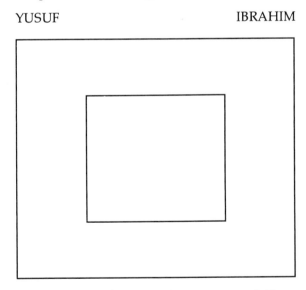

Compare your completed frames with a partner and discuss how Daniel Farson's feelings differ towards the two men. You might also like to consider which of the two men he seems to prefer and why.

3   Here are three possible openings to 'Two Guides to Turkey':

Opening 1

During my stay in Turkey I was lucky to have two guides to show me around this fascinating country. Both in their own distinctive ways were excellent at their job. The first was the multi-talented yet arrogant Yusuf; the second was the quietly knowledgeable, compassionate Ibrahim.

Opening 2

'I am number one man in Istanbul,' Yusuf informed me when we left the tourist office after he had been chosen as my guide. 'Twenty per cent of Istanbul knows me. I do not know them. Funny! My mother was a countess, my father was a count, I am son-of-a-gun.'

'You certainly are,' I agreed.

Opening 3

One of the great pleasures of travel is the relationships you make during your stay abroad. Though such relationships may not last, terminating with that final farewell and the obligatory promise to keep in touch, they can provide memories which will endure for ever. Can I ever forget Yusuf and Ibrahim, my guides during my stay in Turkey? I think not.

With a partner discuss the following questions:

a) What must a writer do in his or her opening paragraph?
b) Which of these openings is the more effective?
c) How can you justify your selection?

Coursework assignments

1   Write two obituaries – one for each character – which celebrate the personalities and lives of these two guides.

2   Imagine that you are Daniel Farson and that you have been asked to write a reference for each of these men for the post described in the advert on page 71.

Write the two references. You should try to cover the following:

- strengths and weaknesses
- personality
- ability as a guide
- suitability for the post.

3   Write a report for a tabloid newspaper describing Ibrahim's meeting with Prince Rainier and Princess Grace.

AFRICA

Tuning into the text

Are you superstitious?

This fun quiz will help you find out just how superstitious you are. Select the answer that comes closest to your reaction to each of the situations described.

1 It's New Year's Eve, and a dark-haired neighbour carrying a lump of coal knocks on the door at midnight. Do you

   a) set your Rottweiler on him?
   b) welcome him in and thank him for coming?
   c) tell him he's too late, carol singers should have come last week?

2 You are helping your parents move home. You are asked to pack the mirrors and pictures that hang on the wall. As you take a mirror off the hook above the mantelpiece, it slips out of your hand, falls into the grate and smashes into a thousand pieces. Do you

   a) hide the pieces and hope your parents don't notice?
   b) nip out to the shops and buy a new one?
   c) lock yourself in your new bedroom for the next seven years?

3 Your mum serves you a boiled egg for breakfast. With the empty shell do you

   a) paint a face on it and use it as head for a glove puppet?
   b) smash it into pieces so no witch can use it as a boat?
   c) put it in the dustbin?

4   At school some workmen are repairing the roof and to go through the main entrance you have to walk under their ladder. Do you

    a) refuse to enter the school until the Head has had the ladder moved?

    b) climb in through the nearest window?

    c) don't notice because you've suddenly remembered the homework you haven't done?

5   Digging in your garden you find an ancient, rusty horseshoe. Do you

    a) nail it to your bedroom door, ends up to keep the lucky power in?

    b) use it as a missile for the black cat that keeps coming into your garden?

    c) put it safely in the shed in case you acquire a horse one day?

6   When giving you your change, a local fish and chip shop owner knocks a salt container over, spilling salt into your open carton of chips. Do you

    a) insist he serves you a fresh carton of chips?

    b) suggest he throws three pinches of salt over his left shoulder into the face of the evil spirit who made him so careless?

    c) ask him for a free go on the fruit machine?

7   Getting dressed in the morning you put a sock on inside out. Do you

    a) immediately correct your mistake?

    b) leave it as it is and hope no one notices?

    c) leave it as it is and expect your premium bond to come up that day?

8   The pavement in front of your house is in a bad state of repair. There is scarcely a paving stone without a crack. As you walk to a friend's house, do you

    a) avoid stepping on the cracks in case a bear will jump out and eat you up?

    b) make a mental note that you must ask your parents to write to the Council?

    c) take special care in case you fall over and ruin your new 501s?

9 You're doing the drying up for your parents and as you place the knives in the drawer, the blades of two knives cross. Do you

   a) not notice because you hate drying up and want to get it done as quickly as possible?
   b) rearrange them because you like things to look neat?
   c) start preparing yourself for the quarrel you know you're going to have with your brother or sister who is helping you?

10 You're sitting in a friend's house, when their black cat comes into the room and leaps up onto your lap. Do you

   a) stroke it and whisper a thank you into its ear?
   b) take it by the scruff of the neck and put it out of the window, because you hate having cat fur over your clothes?
   c) run out of the room sneezing because you're allergic to cats?

For your personal assessment see page 86.

Now in a group discuss these statements. Do you find them true or false?

- Some superstitions are based on common sense
- All superstition is nonsense
- Superstitions are stronger in primitive societies
- People who are superstitious are basically insecure
- People are less superstitious than they used to be
- People make their own luck.

Now read the following article.

CHAMELEONS

Edward Theberton

Tanzania

We went down to our regional capital last week. Fortunately, a break in the rains had made the road passable, at least to a Land-Rover. At the height of the rains it can take up to two weeks to drive the 60 miles or so.

   We gave a lift to a colonel and three of his men, two of whom carried Uzi sub-machine guns. (Although Teacher Nyerere officially supports the PLO and swears eternal solidarity with Yasser Arafat in the hope of handouts from the oil states of the Middle East, he evidently prefers Uzis to Kalashnikovs.) The colonel and his men were accompanying a prisoner on a charge of armed robbery, a slightly crestfallen youth who belonged to a notorious local gang of criminals who usually bought their immunity from prosecution by sharing the booty with the police. For some reason, which the youth did not understand, the system had broken down, and he, a minor member of the gang, had been captured.

About halfway to our destination, I noticed a bright green chameleon crossing the deeply rutted red mud road. It crossed hesitantly, each step preceded by a series of ambivalent rocking movements. I stopped the vehicle, thinking the chameleon would make a nice gift for a small expatriate boy I knew who had recently been devastated by the loss of his white rabbit, which had escaped the hutch and wandered into the African bush, where he might be presumed not to have survived very long.

I picked up the chameleon, a splended prehistoric monster in miniature, with swivelling turret eyes, a scaly ruff around his neck which he flapped when handled, and a gaping mouth with a lower row of teeth that would have been formidable had he been the size of *Tyrannosaurus.* I put my brave little monster on to a copy of the *Times Literary Supplement* which I happened to have with me, and he changed almost at once from his emerald green to the black and white of newsprint, with a few faint yellow stripes. His tail curled into a tight coil.

As I approached the Land-Rover with my captive, the colonel jumped out and ran 50 yards down the road though he was, by African standards, no longer young. The men with their machine guns drew back and cowered, terrified of the small creature, the whites of their eyes standing out against their dark skins, beads of sweat appearing on their brows.

I coaxed the colonel back into the waiting vehicle, though he came only after an assurance that I would keep the chameleon safe by me. As we continued on our journey, I asked my assistant why Africans were so afraid of these harmless reptiles.

'Me, I am not afraiding,' he said proudly, although I later observed that he refused to touch the chameleon, or even to come near it.

At first, they all denied their self-evident terrors; but gradually they revealed their reasons. Each had his own.

'If a chameleon gets in your hair,' said one, 'it never gets out again.'

'The tongue of the chameleon is poison,' said another. 'Otherwise, how could it catch flies?'

'The bite of the chameleon never heals.'

'If a chameleon grips your skin it can never let go, unless the sister of your father does magic.'

I demonstrated the falseness of some of these propositions by allowing the chameleon to crawl all over me. My companions looked on with horrified fascination, but their terrors were too deep-rooted to be removed by my naively rationalist gesture. I felt they were concealing the true, possibly magical significance of chameleons from me, but I was not anthropologist enough to discover it.

A discussion of snakes not surprisingly followed, and I was given a useful hint about what to do in the event of being encoiled by a python. I must take several bamboo poles, and while the snake wraps itself round me I must break the poles with a sharp snap. This will lead the python to suppose that my ribs are cracking, and consequently he will relax his grip to eat me.

I pointed out a few objections to the theory – for instance, that snakes cannot hear, that constrictors do not crush their prey but merely prevent them from inhaling, and that in any case no one had ever been attacked by a python – but what could I be expected to know of Africa after a few months' residence, compared with people whose ancestors had lived there since the beginning of the world?

It was then that one of my companions had the clever idea of putting irrational fear to good use. He suggested that we place the chameleon on the prisoner to make him squeal. The prisoner did not much care for this idea, a form of torture that would leave no traces. He was saved from his ordeal by the fear the guards themselves had of the chameleon, which prevented them from lifting it on to him.

We reached our destination safely, in spite of our accursed passenger. The mother of the little boy for whom I had intended it was playing bridge with three other expatriate ladies, over tea.

'I don't want it in the house,' she said. 'The Africans regard them as unlucky, and there must be something in it.'

'I saw a more beautiful one this morning,' said another of the ladies. 'It was green all over.'

'They go black whenever they're angry or afraid,' said the third.

'And if you put them on a patch of blue,' said the last, 'they get so confused they lie down and die.'   *5 January, 1985*

Views from Abroad
The Spectator Book of Travel Writing (Collins, 1989)

Responding to the text

After you have carefully read 'Chameleons' by Edward Theberton discuss with your teacher which activities to try from the following selection.

1   Theberton emerges as a very different person from his African hosts. Re-read the story carefully and then decide which of the words in this box describe most accurately Theberton and the African soldiers.

Theberton   The soldiers

| reserved   cowardly |
| kind   dishonest   bullying |
| superstitious   rational |
| corrupt   cruel   proud |
| irrational   phlegmatic |
| sympathetic   humble |

_____

_____

_____

_____

_____

_____

Now look at Theberton's account of the expatriate ladies' response to the chameleon. Expatriates are Europeans who have made their home in a foreign country. In this case Africa.

Look at the words in the box again. Which words best describe them?

The expatriate ladies

_____

_____

_____

_____

How can you account for the fact that their reaction to the chameleon is more like that of the African soldiers?

2   Imagine Theberton's account of his encounter with the chameleon forms part of a TV documentary on Africa.

Using a framework like the one below, plan with a partner how you would have filmed this sequence. Make your film as true to the written account as possible in terms of content and effect. Use as many frames as you need.

You may find it helpful to use some film jargon as a form of shorthand:

pan   the camera takes in the landscape or action by sweeping from left to right or from foreground to background or vice versa

track   the camera moves alongside a moving object

close up   the screen is filled with a small detail of the subject of the picture

zoom in/out the camera moves from a wide angle shot to a close up or vice versa

wide angle   the camera sees a large portion of the scene

full frame   the screen is filled with the subject of the picture

half frame   the screen is filled with half of the subject of the picture.

Frame	Sketch	Reference	Camera Instructions	Desired Effect
1		We went down to our regional capital.	Track passage of Land Rover through landscape.	a) to establish setting b) to show effect of rain.

3   As a group discuss your ideas in response to the following questions.

a) How does Theberton wish us to react to his description of the Africans' response to the chameleon?

b) How would you describe Theberton's response to the chameleon?

c) What sort of person is Theberton?

d) Is Theberton sympathetic to Africans and African culture?

e) What does Theberton wish to demonstrate about Africa through his account of the chameleon incident?

f) How would you describe the tone Theberton adopts in this account?

Coursework assignments

1   Conduct your own research into superstitions. You can, if you wish, focus your research on local superstitions or on the general subject. Use the outcome of your research to produce one of the following:

- an article suitable for a teenage magazine
- a factual account suitable for a children's encyclopaedia
- an article for a tabloid newspaper entitled 'Are you Superstitious?'

2 Continue Theberton's account. Imagine that the little boy for whom the writer has brought the chameleon arrives home, sees the reptile and pleads with his mother to keep it. Write the story from Theberton's point of view. Try to bring out

- the various reactions to the chameleon Theberton describes in the account you have read
- Theberton's character
- the nature of the chameleon
- the nature of the Africans.

3 Using the ideas contained in Theberton's account, write a story for young African children entitled *The Chameleon*. Use text and illustration.

Scores and personal assessment for the quiz on pages 79–81

Scores:

1.	A: 0	B: 2	C: 0	6.	A: 0	B: 2	C: 0
2.	A: 0	B: 0	C: 2	7.	A: 0	B: 0	C: 2
3.	A: 0	B: 2	C: 0	8.	A: 2	B: 0	C: 0
4.	A: 2	B: 2	C: 0	9.	A: 0	B: 0	C: 2
5.	A: 2	B: 0	C: 0	10.	A: 2	B: 0	C: 0

20–14 It's a surprise that you're in school today. You are so superstitious that you don't want to get up in the morning in case you're the victim of some bad luck. You are loaded down with lucky charms; your fingers are permanently crossed and your friends will tell you that you look anxious all the time. At the end of each day you thank your lucky stars that you've survived, but one day you just know that . . .

12–6 You're not quite sure about superstition. Part of you tells you that it's just a load of nonsense; the other part of you tells you that there might be something in it and after all, it's better to be safe than sorry. You're the sort of person who will take a lucky mascot into an exam just in case it helps. However, you'll keep it hidden and won't tell anybody.

4–0 You're the down-to-earth type. You won't believe in anything unless you've seen it or experienced it yourself. You think that you have total control over your life and things will only happen if you make them happen yourself.

CHINA

Tuning into the text

Have you ever thought why misunderstandings between people happen? Why do individuals and sometimes groups find it difficult to get on with one another?

The diagram below offers some possible factors that can affect relationships:

wealth

education

beliefs/values

prejudice

language

perception

disability

culture

age

gender

social class

With a partner try to explain how each of these factors can affect relationships and how such factors can cause problems.

Can you think of any factors not listed here?

Now with your partner improvise a selection of scenes each of which shows how one of these factors can cause a disagreement or misunderstanding between two characters.

Polish your most successful scene and present it to your class or a small group.

Set your audience the challenge of working out what it is that is causing the disagreement or misunderstanding.

Discuss your scene with them, using the following ideas as a basis.

- How did the misunderstanding reveal itself?
- How did each of the characters feel during the scene?
- What was the reason for the misunderstanding?
- How could the misunderstanding have been avoided?
- What could each of the characters have done to overcome the misunderstanding?

Now read the following article.

 **FLYING TO CHINA**

Colin Thubron

After the short night, the sun rose upon a country of such desolate strangeness that the woman sitting beside me leaned forward with her hands tensed over her stomach and let out a constricted 'Ohhh!' For three hours we sat craning at the aeroplane window while the snow-peaks of the Karakoram and the western Himalaya glimmered and died among camel-coloured mountains, the mountains merged into hills, and the hills burrowed at last into the Taklimakan Depression, the deepest waterless region on earth. For a while to the north the blades of the Tian Shan range erupted from cushions of cloud, turned pink and harmless by the climbing sun. Then these too vanished, and we were flying along the southern fringes of Mongolia and the Gobi desert. And still, in this country of a quarter of mankind, we saw no sign of life.

Her nation's vastness seemed slightly to have appalled the woman. She said: 'Are you travelling *alone*?'

She was young, conventionally pretty. Only her stained teeth suggested some history poorer than her dress. She wondered where I was going in China, and – covertly – why.

But I could scarcely answer why. The opening-up of China had stirred me unbearably. It was like discovering a new room in a house in which you'd lived all your life. Five years ago the country had been almost inaccessible. Today nearly the whole land could be penetrated by a traveller going alone. More than two hundred and fifty different regions and cities had fallen open, and the traffic of trains, boats and buses between them offered ways of vanishing into the wilds. I

---

dreamed of criss-crossing classical China (no Tibet, no Manchuria) almost at random, of penetrating the tribal regions abutting Burma along the Mekong river, of reaching the eastern Himalaya and following the Great Wall to its end in the far north-west.

But to the woman I only said, a little ashamed (since no Chinese could see so much of her country): 'I want to visit Peking and Shanghai, and maybe I'll go up the Yangtse, then to Canton and . . .'

She smiled her set smile. Perhaps she was wondering what the foreigner could ever understand of her nation – this Westerner with his boorish rucksack (I'd dropped it on her feet) and his failure to travel in a group. What could he ever learn?

Even in childhood – the time of intense, isolated images – my ideas of China had been contradictory and distorted. Its colours then were cold and subtle. It lay embalmed in distance and exotic etiquette. Chinese atrocities were chattered about at my prep school, during the Korean War. 'Have you heard the latest Chinese torture?' my class-mates would demand, before twisting somebody's arm or neck in a novel direction. The Chinese, after all, were stunted and yellow and looked alike. Their multitudinous numbers lent them anonymity. They weren't quite human. Yet for me their landscape resolved into a mist of waterfalls and twisted pines – the Shangri-la of the scroll-paintings – and the idea of a Chinaman harboured a paradoxical element of the ridiculous (something to do with pigtails and *The Nutcracker Suite*, I think). In any case, China was too distant to be threatening. It was – and remained – a luminous puzzle.

People's images of countries are rich in such buried sediment, which goes on haunting long after experience or common sense has diluted it. And by now – as we floated above the wrung-out steppes of the Gobi – other strata had overlaid the first. In the anarchy of the Cultural Revolution, between 1966 and 1976, the Chinese people had not merely been terrorised from above but had themselves – tens of millions of them – become the instruments of their own torture. The land had sunk into a peculiar horror. A million were killed; some 30 million more were brutally persecuted, and unknown millions starved to death. Yet it was less the numbers which appalled than the refinements of cruelty practised – in one province alone 75 different methods of torture were instituted – and I never thought of the country now without being dogged by a tragic question mark.

The woman was rummaging in her handbag. In the seats behind us a conclave of Peking businessmen sprawled, their shirt-collars open, their eyes closed. I was seized by the foolish idea that each one of them was withholding some secret from me – some simple, perfect illumination. Because that is the foreigner's obsession in this country. At every moment, round every corner, the question 'Who are they?' erupts and nags. How could they be so led? How could they do what they had done? And had they ever changed – this people of exquisite poetry and refined brush-strokes, and pitilessness? A billion un-comprehended people.

Beneath us now, were the last hills tilted south-eastward out of Inner Mongolia into the huge alluvial basin of the Yellow River, I could see the divide between plateau and plain, agricultural hardship and sufficiency, drawn vertically down the earth's atlas with the precision of a pencil-line. To the west brown, to the east green.

Within half an hour we would be landing in Peking, and as if these last airborne minutes might liberate us from inhibitions I started talking with the woman about the Cultural Revolution. She turned quizzically to me and asked: 'What do you think of Mao Tse-tung in the West?' I said we thought him a remarkable leader, but inhumane. She said coldly: 'Yes. He made mistakes.'

Mistakes! He had caused more than 20 million deaths. Sometimes he had acted and talked about people as if they were mere disposable counters on an ideological gameboard. And she talked of mistakes! It was how the Russians spoke of Stalin. I said tightly – I felt this might be my last (and first) chance to vent anger in China: 'Mistakes! All that suffering inflicted on your people! How can you forgive that?' Then I added: 'I think he became a monster.'

She went quiet and stared somewhere beyond me. The fact did not seem to have occurred to her before. Then she said simply: 'Yes.'

For some reason I felt ashamed. Whatever she meant by her 'Yes', its tone – distant, as if admitting something irrelevant – signalled that I did not understand. She fastened her seat-belt. I said: 'Of course it's hard for us in the West to imagine . . .'

Us in the West. We must seem outlandish, I thought, with our garish self-centredness, our coarse opulence, our sentimentality. Somebody had told me that the Chinese found our big feet and noses preposterous, and that to them we smelt. The next moment I had asked the woman penitently: 'Do we smell?'

Her fragile face smiled back at me. 'Yes, of course.'

I baulked. 'Very much?'

'Oh yes. All the time.'

I supposed that her bemused smile was there to cover embarrass-ment. But I asked finally, edging a little away: 'Do I smell?'

'Yes.'

It was too late to go back now. 'What of?'

'What?'

'What of? What do I smell of?'

'Oh!' She plunged her face into her hands in a sudden paroxysm of giggles. '*Smell.* I thought you said *smile!*' The tinkle and confusion of her laughter sabotaged the next few sentences, then she said: 'Only in the summer. Westerners sweat more than Chinese. That's all, that's all. No, you don't . . . smell. No, really . . . no.'

We were coming in to land.   *25 January, 1986*

Views from Abroad
The Spectator Book of Travel Writing (Collins, 1989)

Responding to the text

After you have carefully read 'Flying to China' by Colin Thubron, discuss with your teacher which activities to try from the following selection:

1   Read the text again and as you read note down any moments of mis-understanding.

Now go back and examine the reasons for the misunderstanding. See if you can categorise them using the words given to you in the list on p. 87.

Compare your list with your partner and discuss your answers.

2   Many of the examples of travel writing in this book have been taken from *The Spectator.*

Imagine you are the editor of *The Spectator* and Thubron has sent you 'Flying to China'. Although you like the piece, it is too long for you to be able to use it all. You have to cut it by a third.

What would you cut out of the article?

Before you make your cuts you need to make a list of your criteria – that is, the basis on which you are going to reduce the article in length.

When you have finished, compare your cuts and your criteria with those of the rest of your group. Decide who has completed the task most successfully.

These questions might help you make your decision.

a) Have any of the cuts damaged the sense of the piece?
b) What was the most important moment in the piece? How would you justify the selection you have chosen as the most important moment? Has the editor retained that moment?
c) Is there anything in the article that does not contribute to the main idea in the piece? Has the editor retained or cut that section?
d) Has the piece still got a clear structure?

3 Improvise Thubron's flight to China. You will need three other people:

- one member of the group will play the part of Thubron
- one will play Thubron's thoughts
- one will play the part of the Chinese woman
- and one will play her thoughts.

You will need to plan this scene carefully and practise it to get the timing right.

Compare your improvisation with another group's. Were there any differences in interpretation of the characters?

How do you account for those differences? Do they give you an insight into what Thubron is saying through his account of his flight to China?

Coursework assignments

1 Write a narrative in which a misunderstanding arising from one of the factors listed on page 87 plays a vital part.

2 One of the aims of schools is to promote better understanding between different races and cultures. Produce a report which sets out positive steps schools could take to create this better understanding. Take care to justify each recommendation you make.

3 Write a book review of any book that you have read that has given you a better insight into the culture of another country. You might try one or two of the following titles, if you have not read any multicultural books before:

Things Fall Apart Chinua Achebe
A Walk in the Night Alex La Guma
Weep Not Child Ngugi Wa Thiongo
God's Bits of Wood Sembene Ousmane

Green Days by the River Michael Antony
Crick Crack Monkey Merle Hodge
Short Stories from India, Pakistan and Bangladesh ed. Ranjana Ash
Best West Indian Stories ed. Kenneth Ramchand
A Bend in the Ganges Manohar Malgonkar
How Many Miles to Babylon? Paula Fox
Native Son Richard Wright
Roll of Thunder, Hear My Cry Mildred Taylor
Another Country James Baldwin
The Siege of Babylon Farrukh Dhondy

Or you could try any of the travel writing listed at the end of this book in the Further Reading section.

JAMAICA

Tuning into the text

Read this poem by a London schoolgirl:

A LETTER TO JO IN JAMAICA

The wind blows sweetly
in long summer days
you tell me and involve me.

Colourful fish come
from boats on
the sea shore, every day.

I wake up in dark
and misty mornings
half the year.

You have sunshine, sunshine
the flame tree echoing
and the nightingale.

You eat food
with sugar and spices.
I eat mashed potatoes.

I stand in heavy clothes
against my skin.
You go about light, golden brown
like polished mahogany.

Joan Davidson, City Lines
(ILEA English Centre, 1982)

- With a partner draw up a list of five questions which will help you discover the full meaning of this poem when answered.
- Exchange your questions with another pair.
- With your partner discuss the answers to the questions that you have been given.
- Using your answers to these questions prepare a short commentary on the poem which attempts to set out its meaning clearly.
- Exchange commentaries with the same pair; read the commentary you have received carefully and discuss it critically with the writers, challenging any points you disagree with.

Now as you read 'No Refuge for Rastas' try to compare Joan Davidson's view of life in Jamaica with that presented by Zenga Longmore.

 **NO REFUGE FOR RASTAS**

Zenga Longmore

After a week in Jamaica, I was so convinced I was in hell that I found myself wondering when I had died and what I had done to deserve such terrible retribution.

The scorching heat was to me the flames of Hades, the inflamed mosquito bites were the plague of boils, and the misery on the faces 5
of the poverty-striken people was surely the mark of souls in torment.

I was not dead, however. I was alive and well and staying in a small Clarendon town, for a month's holiday, with my sister, brother-in-law and his family. The house in which we were living was a huge bedraggled, home for armies of ants, cockroaches, giant spiders, rats, 10
bats, nine children, and eight adults.

I would escape into the towns occasionally, but this was difficult, owing to the lack of transport. There is no public transport in Jamaica, only privately owned minibuses, with such fierce competition that the drivers grab you, shouting: 'Kingston! Mandeville! Spanish Town!' 15
The strongest of the lot will seize you and frogmarch you towards a tiny minibus, packed solid with people. 'B-but I don't want to go to Kingston!' you protest as you are wedged in between a tight-lipped old lady and a basket of green bananas. 'Is where you a-go?' 'May Pen!' But it's too late. The bus boggles down the road at breakneck 20
speed. Evil Knievel is the idol of the Jamaican driver. The bus finally deposits you at a remote town, leaving you almost too dazed to inquire how to get to where you first wanted to go.

The towns are crumbling away in a heap of decay. Every Jamaican

between 16 and 50 feels that Jamaica is merely a transit land, which 25
one has to put up with until one can get to England or America.
Because of this Jamaica is unloved. No one bothers to make a go of the
good life there: instead of building up a better Jamaica, Jamaicans
merely save up every penny they can earn, and shoot off to England or
the States, leaving bitter wives, husbands and children behind. Build- 30
ings that were once grand and gleaming, stand peeling and filthy,
surrounded by foul refuse. The shops, such as they are, sell the barest
utility foods. Dead dogs lie in the gutter, their insides strewn on the
pavements.

People just stand, waiting for nothing. They stared at my sister and 35
me with blank, shuttered faces, muttering, 'Foreigners,' as we passed.
It took me a while to realise that we were not being insulted. It is a
statement; we are not Jamaican (although black), so we come from
'foreign'.

Everywhere I went I saw children: children who don't play, child- 40
ren who stand or sit motionless. Families are large, and yet there are
very few facilities for children. I saw no playgrounds, and few toy-
shops. The school I visited was a swarming mass of impeccably
dressed children standing three to a desk, copying off the blackboard.
The teacher stood at the front of the class glaring, strap in hand. When 45
I asked to see a ten-year-old's book he showed me a page of beautiful
Victorian italic writing, all about the English Queen.

'What does it say?' I asked.

He looked at me blankly.

'Read some out to me.' 50

'Me nar read,' he said.

Jamaican schools appeared to be a showcase of immaculate uni-
forms and copying, but no teaching. I came across no child under the
age of 14 who had the first clue concerning reading and writing. The
adults didn't blame the schools. They blamed Jamaica itself. 'It jus' 55
dat foreign pickney dem is clever,' I was often told.

The people had a touching love of England. The grannies, who
dominate Jamaican life, sat around telling their families that England
is the mother country, and Jamaica her daughter. My sister and I were
treated as English duchesses. We were not allowed to do our own 60
washing or washing up. 'You's a lady, so you mustn't get your hands
dirty,' we were told, as we were dragged away from the sink. Our
accents and 'high gold' complexions were a passport to having first
place in any queue, and a seat on the buses. It felt most odd to be
treated like English royalty in Jamaica after a lifetime of not being 65
considered English in England.

White people were neither here nor there, but 'fair-skinned' black people were guaranteed posh jobs and affected snobby mannerisms. I was considered inordinately rich, and received more offers of marriage in my first week than ever before in my life. Once I was taken to see a prospective mother-in-law, an old lady living in the Blue Mountains in a one-roomed wooden shack, along with six grandchildren and a frail old husband. There was no gas or electricity, only kerosene lamps and a firewood cooker. The water was supplied by a stream half a mile away.

'Please marry my son, ma'am. Tek him to Englan' and mak him rich.' I glanced at the gormless young man, and told her I'd have to think it over. Then I took a long, pensive walk back to the nearest town.

The scenery was the most beautiful I have ever laid eyes upon. Lush palms and banana trees, and exotic flowers, all in vivid colours. Fabulous mountains, rivers, gorges and lakes. Sitting on a rock by a waterfall in the Blue Mountains, I realised that what I had mistaken for hell was in fact paradise.

Then I began to notice the implicit honesty of the people. No one ever swindled, mistrusted, or cheated me. Market traders left their wares unattended, and shoppers would pick up the goods, and leave the right amount of money by the side of the stalls. Even in Kingston, that great sprawling town of incomparable ugliness, I never felt unsafe, even when alone at night. Because of Kingston's violent reputation, nobody walked the streets, so there wasn't anyone around to be violent. Just street after street of dilapidated houses, empty shops, and vile refuse. Festering on the outskirts of Kingston were forlorn shanty shacks, lying higgledy-piggledy in muddy pathways. They are built of wood, corrugated iron, barrel lids – anything that will keep out the tropical rainstorms. The goats and dogs of these shanty towns seem as miserable and apathetic as the people.

On my last day in Jamaica, my relations finally succeeded in dragging me to a church. The family members who didn't come were bowed down with guilt and apologies. Everyone goes to church in Jamaica; only the 'quashie dem' don't go. ('Quashie' are the lumpen-proletariat, the hoi polloi; 'dem' being the plural. Plurals and tenses are few and far between in Jamaica.)

The church was an enormous hall, crammed with hundreds of people, grannies, grandads, mums, dads, and kids. Our party could only get a seat by virtue of 'coming from foreign', but hundreds of others stood round the hall, packed solid against the walls. White hats and lace dresses sparked in the sunshine. The singing was lovely,

sweet voices harmonising soulful gospel music. Then the preacher
began her sermon, shouting into a microphone about the Devil and 110
his cunning ways. I am afraid I am unable to elaborate on the speech,
because I promptly nodded off to sleep.

I was awoken with a jerk by a sharp nudge in the ribs. 'Wake!
Wake! Preacher she say would foreign lady stand up.' I stood up,
swaying slightly on my feet. The preacher smiled at me. 'It nice to 115
have English miss in our congregation. Welcome.' I smiled goofily
back, and the service went on. Thousands of people singing and
banging tambourines.

Church services sprang up impromptu wherever I went. In busy
market places a spontaneous preacher would leap up and begin to
declaim the Bible to the masses. Shoppers crowded around, and 120
listened avidly to his sermon.. Amens rent the air. Then singing of
pure beauty filled the thronging market, and I found myself swept
along with the religious fervour, shouting and clapping.

Steal away, steal away, steal away to Jesus

Steal away, steal away home, I ain't got long to stay here.   125

All the energy in Jamaica seems to have gone into the churches, the
creation of the slaves, a force much stronger than materialism. Maybe
this has something to do with the honesty and humility which radiate
from the people, especially the young people. There are no 'teenagers'
in Jamaica. People under the age of 18 are children, and anyone over 130
is an adult. This means that, thank goodness, there are no gangs of
youths in Jamaica, who stand on street corners, smoking and shouting
abuse at passers-by. I was amazed to find that reggae is hardly heard.
It is looked down upon as a rough music, like punk rock, music of the
quashie dem. Any self-respecting Jamaican will listen to Jim Reeves, 135
and Sixties ballads. Rastas are a rare sight. They are considered
godless backsliders, who are prayed for in church by their weeping
relatives.

When I told a middle-aged lady that London is simply stuffed with
reggae and Rastas, she shuddered and gasped: 'And I allowed my 140
Errol to live in that wicked place!' I didn't tell her that I had imagined
Jamaica to be a Rasta haven, with reggae parties blaring from every
house. Far from it; Jamaica is not a young person's country. Night-
clubs are empty, save for a handful of middle-aged men, and young
men keep well in the background. The image of violent Jamaican 145
youth is instantly dispelled on seeing the somewhat gauche young
men who are too much in awe of the bossy old grannies to speak.

The young girls were more assertive, relentlessly begging me to
send for them when I returned to England. Because they would not

take no for an answer, I ummed and ahhed until my last day.   150
    I left Jamaica with a feeling that it is heaven and hell combined. As I
sped through Kingston's ruinous streets for the last time, I had a
conviction that something must be done fast, but what? Somebody
has to do something to make Jamaicans love Jamaica, land of the
world's most exquisite scenery and of careworn religious people. 155

22 November, 1986

Views from Abroad
The Spectator Book of Travel Writing (Collins, 1989)

Responding to the text

After you have carefully read 'No Refuge for Rastas' by Zenga Longmore
discuss with your teacher which activities to try from the following selection.

1   Imagine that Zenga Longmore is given the opportunity to commission a
    professional photographer to take five photographs to illustrate this
    article.

    She gives the photographer strict instructions using the framework
    below. In the box on the left-hand side she draws a rough sketch of the
    scene; in the space below the sketch she has written the caption she
    wishes to use; and in the box on the right she describes the content of the
    photograph and the effect she wishes each photograph to have.

	Details: _____
	_____
	_____
	_____
	_____
	_____
	Effect: _____
	_____
Caption:	_____
	_____

2   During the course of this piece Zenga Longmore's feelings about Jamaica change quite considerably. Look at the graph opposite.

  a) Which of the three lines on the graph represents most accurately the change in Zenga Longmore's feelings? Copy the graph with the line you feel most appropriate. If you feel that none of them is suitably accurate, draw your own line.

  b) Now choose the five experiences in Zenga Longmore's visit that most influence her feelings about Jamaica. Mark those points on the graph and annotate them, explaining clearly which experience each of the five points along your chosen line stands for.

  c) Compare your graph with that of a partner. Discuss the differences. Justify your selection and challenge your partner's selection.

3   Imagine that Jamaica is about to hold elections for their government. You and a group of friends decide to form your own political party. Give it an appropriate name, and using your reading of 'No Refuge for Rastas', formulate a set of policies which aim to encourage more Jamaicans to stay and enjoy life in their own country.

  a) Produce your manifesto which briefly sets out your policies.
  b) Exchange your manifesto with that of another group.
  c) Study their manifesto and look for weaknesses in their policies and points which you disagree with.

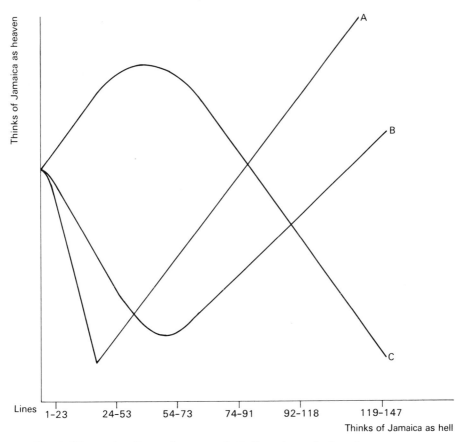

Graph illustrating Zenga Longmore's feelings towards Jamaica

d) Appoint two spokespersons from your group to represent your party on a *Question Time* panel. Members of the audience will ask the representatives on the panel about their policies. Your spokespersons will have the opportunity to explain your party's policies and attack the policies of the rival party. The resulting debate will be controlled by an impartial chairperson.

Coursework assignments

1   Bearing in mind your work in Task 3 go on to produce a range of campaign literature. This might include any of the following:

- posters
- a speech
- the redrafted manifesto

- a campaign leaflet
- an acceptance speech on the occasion of your victory
- a transcript of an interview with your candidate
- a newspaper article on your candidate and his or her party's views.

2   If you can, interview someone you know who has emigrated (where from doesn't matter) and find out if life in Britain was what they expected it to be.

Use the results of your research to write *one* of the following.

a) A narrative called *The Immigrant*.
b) An extract from an imaginary autobiography setting out the experiences of an immigrant.
c) A three-minute script for a radio programme on the experience of emigration, perhaps using actual quotes from your interviewee.

3   Write a series of letters exchanged between a Jamaican who has emigrated and his family back home. Try to bring out the difference in their present lifestyle from the one they had in Jamaica and focus on whether or not the Jamaican's expectations about life abroad have been fulfilled.

FOLLOW UP ASSIGNMENTS

Having explored travel writing through attempting some of the activities in this book, it is now time to reflect on what you have learnt. The following activities will produce coursework material appropriate for your GCSE English folders. In order to complete these tasks successfully you will have to think carefully about what you have read and done. You might find it helpful to re-read the pieces you have enjoyed and to refer back to some of the work you have completed.

It is not suggested that you attempt all of these tasks. Choose the task which most appeals to you and discuss your choice with your teacher before starting.

1   Discuss with the librarian in your school the possibility of launching a campaign to promote travel writing amongst fellow pupils. This campaign might include all our some of the following:

   - lunchtime readings of travel literature
   - a display
   - a booklet of fellow pupils' reviews of appropriate travel writing
   - posters promoting travel writing or individual travel writers
   - an art display of work in response to pieces of travel writing
   - a visit from a travel writer who may be asked to give a talk or run a workshop
   - a display of pupil travel writing.

2   Choose a particular travel writer whose work you have responded to. Try corresponding with them. Write a letter to them describing your response to their texts that you have read.

3   Choose one of the writers from this collection and try to find other travel writing by them, or choose one or more texts by the same writer from the reading list on page 106.

   After you have read some more articles, or a full length travel book by your chosen writer, produce your own personal study. This study should try to fulfil the following objectives:

   - give a clear indication of the content of the works you have read
   - describe the writer's attitude and/or response to his subjects
   - identify your own personal interest in his or her work
   - justify a recommendation to other students.

4   Try your hand at travel writing. One of the aims of this collection is to illustrate the range of form and purpose of travel writing.

Use this planner to help you think about your piece. Choose *one* or more elements from each column.

Place	*Focus*	*Purpose*	*Audience*
building	person	amuse	general reader
street	people	inform	teenagers
town	group	reflect	under 12s
village	race	provoke thought	adults
area	culture	persuade	pensioners
country	customs	promote	
continent	mannerisms	entertain	
	history	explore	
	landscape/scenery	describe	
	food	evoke	
		narrate	
		criticise	

You should now have some idea about the content of your piece, which you can now develop in detail before you start writing. You should remember that above all you must aim to communicate your personal response to your chosen subject. This response might be either a thought or a feeling or a combination of the two.

If you can, illustrate your travel writing with appropriate photographs and/or drawings.

5   Produce a readers' guide to a selection from the travel writing in this text. Your guide should be aimed at students of your own age and it should

- give the reader a brief indication of the content of each text
- identify the themes of each text
- describe each text's readership appeal, bearing in mind the potential audience
- persuade the potential reader to read the text.

6   If you have the opportunity to travel – whether in Britain or abroad – keep a diary of your experiences. Try to note down your impressions of the people you meet and of the places you visit as well as incidents that happen.

Use this diary later as the basis for producing a piece of developed travel writing.

7   When you have attempted coursework assignments from this text, get together in a group and re-work any pieces of travel writing you have

undertaken, in order to produce an anthology of travel writing by teenagers for teenagers.

Remember this is a group activity. Use members of your group to advise you on how to improve your contribution to the anthology. When discussing your work with other members of your group, you might find these questions helpful:

- What is the aim of the piece?
- Does it fulfil its aim?
- Is it too long? Can anything be omitted to improve the piece?
- Is it too short? What needs to be added and why?
- Has the piece a clear structure – an opening that makes the reader read on? A middle that develops the key ideas/feelings/atmosphere? An ending that rounds the piece off appropriately?
- Does the piece take account of the reader? Does (s)he need more information/detail than the writer has supplied? Is the style suitable? Is any of the expression awkward, muddled, confusing or vague?

If you criticise each other's work, try to be positive. Suggest specific actions the writer can take to improve his or her piece.

Once you are happy with the content, look carefully at the spelling and punctuation.

When you are putting the anthology together, discuss the best order for the material, provide illustrations or appropriate photographs if you can and give it an appropriate title.

8   Arrange an evening for parents on the subject of travel. This evening might consist of any combination of the following:

- readings of professional and pupils' travel writing
- polished improvisations examining aspects of travel
- tape-slide presentations by pupils/staff of trips abroad.

9   Find out what travel writing your local library has in its stock. If you discover that your favourite travel writer is not represented, or if a travel book that you have enjoyed is not in its stock, write to the Chief Librarian recommending the text or writer, setting out clearly your reasons for doing so.

10 Write your own handbook for travel writers entitled *Beginning Travel Writing*. This should include advice regarding how to start, the range of subjects which are suitable and the sort of approaches that might be attempted.

You will also need to provide extracts from examples of effective travel writing to illustrate your points.

FURTHER READING

Bruce Chatwin, *The Songlines*
Jim Corbett, *The Man-Eating Leopard of Rudraprayag*
Lawrence Durrell, *Reflections on a Marine Venus*
Ranulph Fiennes, *To the Ends of the Earth*
John Foster, *Round the World on a Wheel*
John Gale, *Travels with a Son*
Richard Girling (ed.), *The Sunday Times Travel Book Three*
Graham Greene, *Journey Without Maps*
Arthur Grimble, *A Pattern of Islands*
Norman Lewis, *The Volcanoes Above*
Jan Morris, *Journeys, Cities, Travels, Destinations*
Eric Newby, *A Short Walk in the Hindu Kush*
Eric Newby (ed.), *A Book of Travellers' Tales*
Derek Nimmo, *Up Mount Everest Without a Paddle*
P.J. O'Rourke, *Holidays in Hell*
Michael Palin, *Around the World in 80 Days*
Nick Sanders, *The Great Bike Ride (Around the World in 80 Days)*
Robert Falcon Scott, *Scott's Last Expedition: The Personal Journals of Captain R.F. Scott*
Joe Simpson, *Touching the End*
Paul Theroux, *The Great Railway Bazaar*
　　　　　　　Sunrise with Sea Monsters
Colin Thubron, *Behind the Wall*
Laurens van de Post, *Venture to the Interior*
Keith Waterhouse, *The Theory and Practice of Travel*
Gavin Young, *Slow Boat to China*